Sea of Japan

Hokkaidō

Sapporo

$4.00
OVERSEAS
2/17

AOMORI

Aomori

AKITA

Akita

Morioka

IWATE

Chūson-ji
Tendai sect

Sōji-ji
Sōtō sect (Zen)

Sado Island

Sado
Nichiren's second place of exile

YAMAGATA

Yamagata

MIYAGI

Zuigan-ji
Rinzai sect (Zen)

Zenkō-ji

Shinran exiled to north of Japan

Niigata

Sendai

Pacific Ocean

ISHIKAWA

Kanazawa

Toyama

NIIGATA

Fukushima

TOYAMA

Nagano

GIFU

NAGANO

Honshū

Kōfu

GUMMA

Maebashi

TOCHIGI

Utsunomiya

FUKUSHIMA

Rinnō-ji
Tendai sect

Banna-ji
Shingon sect

Hokekyō-ji
Nichiren sect

SAITAMA

YAMANASHI

Urawa

IBARAKI

Mito

Narita-san
Shingon sect

TOKYO

Tōkyō

Chiba

Kawasaki Daishi
Shingon sect

SHIZUOKA

KANAGAWA

Yokohama

Shizuoka

CHIBA

Sōji-ji
Sōtō sect (Zen)

Kiyosumi-dera
Nichiren sect
(Nichiren studied here)

Yakuō-in
Shingon sect

Kominato
Nichiren's birthplace

Itō
Nichiren's first place of exile

KAMAKURA
Kenchō-ji
Rinzai sect (Zen)
Enkaku-ji
Rinzai sect
Jufuku-ji
Rinzai sect
(founder: Eisai)
Tōkei-ji
(Kakekomi-dera)
Rinzai sect
Kōtoku-ji
(Kamakura *daibutsu*)
Jōdo sect

TŌKYŌ
Sensō-ji
Tendai sect
Kan'ei-ji
Tendai sect
Jindai-ji
Tendai sect
Gokoku-ji
Shingon sect
Nishi Arai Daishi
Shingon sect
Zōjō-ji
Jōdo sect
Tsukiji Hongan-ji
Jōdo-Shin sect
Hommon-ji
Nichiren sect
(Nichiren died here)
Sōka Gakkai
Risshō Kōsei-kai
Reiyūkai

BUDDHISM

BUDD

Japan's Cultu

Introduction by **Edwin O. Reischauer**

H I S M
r a l I d e n t i t y

Stuart D. B. Picken

KODANSHA INTERNATIONAL
Tokyo, New York and San Francisco

ACKNOWLEDGMENTS

The author would like to thank Professor Gamō Toshihito of Kokugakuin University and Professor J. Edward Kidder, Jr., for their valuable guidance and comments on the manuscript; the staff of Kodansha International for unfailing courtesy, enthusiastic resourcefulness, and outstanding professionalism; Professor Edwin O. Reischauer for kindly agreeing to write the Introduction; and finally the authorities of the many temples and religious institutions visited over the past decade and the priests and scholars who have offered their erudite views.

NAMES AND TERMS: Most Buddhist names and terms are given in Japanese rather than in Sanskrit except for those like "nirvana" and "bodhisattva," where the Sanskrit word is already established usage in English. The names of Japanese people are given in the Japanese order: family name first, personal name second. *Ji*, *tera*, and *dera* are suffixes meaning "temple."

PHOTO CREDITS: (Numbers in italics refer to color plates, other numbers to pages.) Bon Color Photo Agency, half title, *1*, *6*, *33*, *37*; Dandy Photo, *5*; Ejiri Tamihisa, *31* (by courtesy of Chūō Kōronsha); Fine Photo, *3*, *32*; Fujita Shōichi, *16–19* (by courtesy of Tōsō Co., Ltd), 11; Hirota Naotaka, title, *30*; Japan Times, *40*; Kaneko Keizō, *4*, *21*, *22*, *23*, *27*, *28*, 32, 44; Kōdansha, 7 (by courtesy of Chūgū-ji), *34* (by courtesy of Tōdai-ji), *35* (by courtesy of Hōryū-ji), *36* (by courtesy of Kōya-san, Kongōbu-ji), 12, 25 (by courtesy of Shitennō-ji), 69 (by courtesy of Tō-ji); Kokusai Photo Agency, *8*, *9*, *10*, *11*, *12*, *13*, *14*, *15*, *24*, *25*, *28*, *29*, *38*, 10, 24, 33 (left), 37, 40, 57 (right), 61, 72, 77; Maruyama Isamu, *2*; Nishikawa Isamu, *39*; Pan-Asia Newspaper Alliance, *26*; Risshō Kōsei-kai, *41*, 78; Seibu Department Store, 49 (right); Sōka Gakkai, *42*; Tokyo National Museum, 45, 56 (by courtesy of Kōzan-ji), 57 (left); Tokyo Photo Agency, 20, 27; Waley, Paul, 26, 32, 33 (right), 49 (left), 52, 76.

Picture research and design, Katakura Nobuhiro; editorial work, Paul Waley; maps, Kojima Michio; line drawings on pp. 64, 65, Suzuki Yoshito; drawing on back end-paper, Kuwata Kinji.

Distributed in the United States by Kodansha International/USA Ltd. through Harper & Row, Publishers, Inc., 10 East 53rd Street, New York, New York 10022. Published by Kodansha International Ltd., 12–21, Otowa 2-chome, Bunkyo-ku, Tokyo 112 and Kodansha International/USA Ltd., 10 East 53rd Street, New York, New York 10022 and 44 Montgomery Street, San Francisco, California 94104. Photographs Copyright © 1982 by Kodansha International Ltd. Text Copyright in Japan 1982 by Kodansha International Ltd. All rights reserved. Printed in Japan.

LCC 81-84800
ISBN 0-87011-499-9
ISBN4-7700-0987-9 (in Japan)

CONTENTS

Introduction

Buddhism and Shinto are the two great historic religions of Japan, but at least in origin there could not be two religions less alike. Shinto is purely and completely Japanese. It grows out of the very soil of the land. Since prehistoric times it has been part of the Japanese way of life. Strictly speaking it has no philosophy, and it has no history, except that of the Japanese people as a whole. It is an embodiment of pervasive Japanese attitudes toward life and toward the wonders of nature that surround man. It is hard to imagine Japan without Shinto, and there would be no Shinto without the Japanese people. Shinto is a simple, almost amorphous religion that fits one people—and only one.

Buddhism, by the way of contrast, takes its place beside Christianity and Islam as one of the great international faiths of mankind. Starting in northern India around 500 B.C., it spread southward throughout the subcontinent and to Sri Lanka and Southeast Asia and northward and eastward through Afghanistan, central Asia, and Tibet to China, Korea, and Japan. For a while it touched the greater part of the world's population. In the eighth century images of the Buddha made in the Indian region, Southeast Asia, Java, central Asia, China, Korea, and Japan were so much alike that today they can scarcely be told apart. Buddhism knows no national or cultural boundaries; it is a religion for all men everywhere.

Unlike Shinto with its lack of a clear philosophy, Buddhism was born of complex philosophical attitudes, and as it grew it produced such a broad diversity of thought that one could well imagine that every religious concept possible to man has been embraced somewhere and at some time as an element of Buddhism. In its native India it developed a huge body of scriptures, known as the Tripitaka, or "Three Baskets," written in the Sanskrit and Pali languages. These were translated into other languages, particularly Chinese, which became the basic medium for Japanese Buddhism. The Chinese Tripitaka consists of more than 1,600 works in over 5,000 sections. On the basis of this vast sacred literature, thousands of Buddhist treatises were composed in Japanese and the other new languages of the faith.

In contrast to Shinto, Buddhism has a ponderous history, going back two millenia and a half. At an early time it divided into two major streams. One is Hinayana, or Theravada, which continues as the main line of the monastic form of Buddhism of south Asia. The other is Mahayana, which is the immensely diverse form of Buddhism that spread to China, Korea, and Japan. Mahayana enriched itself by incorporating many of the religious beliefs and practices it found in its new missionary domains and by developing the doctrine that the numerous variations and contradictions to be found in its beliefs are alternate aspects of the same basic truths, given different form to accommodate the varying levels of comprehension and sophistication of the diverse believers in the faith.

At an early time Buddhism developed a rich art and iconography that had an immediate visual appeal to new converts and probably accounts for the success of Buddhism as a great missionary religion almost as much as its ideas. This art became mixed with Greek artistic influences in the area of modern Afghanistan, where semi-Greek kingdoms had been left behind by the conquests of Alexander the Great. It was this Greco-Indian art which spread with Buddhism all the way to the shores of Japan.

The original philosophic concepts of Buddhism were fundamentally pessimistic, contrasting sharply to the simple, almost joyous acceptance of nature and human life that characterized Shinto. It accepted the then-prevalent Indian idea that life was painful and also unending. One life led to the next and through *karma*, a term implying "causality," conditioned its nature. Man was caught in an endless chain of suffering. The great discovery of the historical Buddha, Sakyamuni (Shaka in Japanese), was that this painful chain of *karma* was caused by desires and that it could be broken by the realization of this fact and the suppression of these desires through leading a virtuous life in accordance with the Eightfold Path he advocated. Through it, one could achieve nirvana, described as being like the peaceful merging of a drop of water into the sea.

It is doubtful that such a philosophy alone would have had much appeal to the simple and optimistic Japanese, but Buddhism first came to Japan already much transformed and embellished at the hands of the Chinese. The original historical Buddha, or "Enlightened One," had multiplied into a number of different Buddhas, each with his individual magical characteristics. A new type of deity had also developed called a bodhisattva, who, though an "Enlightened Existence," delayed assuming full buddhahood in order to help his fellowmen to salvation. Nirvana changed from being merely the extinction of the ego and became the attainment of immediate salvation in an appealing paradise like that of the popular Buddha Amida.

Buddhism first seeped into China in the early centuries of the Christian era and reached its apogee there in the eighth century. It was introduced to Japan through Korea in the sixth century, appealing at the time to the Japanese as a new and possibly more powerful form of divine intervention than that of their own Shinto deities. It also came embedded in Chinese civilization and was accepted as an integral part of the art, literature, and thought of China, which Japan imported with great enthusiasm during the next few centuries. A series of official Japanese embassies was dispatched to the Chinese capital between 607 and 838, at the height of the Buddhist age in China, and Buddhist monks and students accompanying these embassies played a leading role in importing Chinese Buddhism to Japan.

Buddhism first found a foothold in Japan at the imperial court, and it took centuries for it to spread outward geographically to all parts of Japan and downward to the ordinary people. It took even longer for Buddhism to become fully acclimated to Japanese society. The early temples and monasteries were largely built by the court, and in the eighth century the emperor Shōmu envisioned a nationwide court-sponsored Buddhist church paralleling the secular government. The Great Buddha of Nara, dedicated in 752, was the chief physical embodiment of this concept. The six prevailing sects of the Nara period (710–93) were all strictly Chinese imports, based on Chinese interpretations of philosophical variations of Buddhism deriving directly from India.

In the ninth century the first long steps were taken toward making Buddhism more congenial to the Japanese people as a whole. Two monks who had accompanied the embassy of 804 to China brought back two more Chinese sects, but these were both more Chinese and less Indian than the earlier sects had been and more attuned to Japanese interests. Kūkai, better known by his posthumous title of Kōbō Daishi, brought back the Shingon school and Saichō the Tendai, named for its mountain headquarters in China. Both placed their home monasteries on mountaintops, hearkening back to the old Japanese identification of the beauties of nature with religious sentiments. Shingon in full and Tendai in part were based on magic formulae and mandalas, pictorial representations of philosophical ideas, which were easy to visualize, even though they might be difficult to comprehend in detail.

The Tendai sect was typically Chinese in its inclusiveness and its organization by categories of almost all the various tendencies within the extraordinarily diverse teachings of Mayahana Buddhism. It carried within it the seeds of most later developments in Japanese Buddhism. It included the worship of Amida as the "Buddha of the Western Paradise" and of the *Lotus Sutra* as promising the salvation of all creatures. It also contained the rudiments of the meditation school of Buddhism, known best by its Japanese name of Zen. Thus the Enryaku-ji, the central monastery of Tendai, high on Mount Hiei above the capital city of Kyoto, became a sort of mother church for most of later Japanese Buddhism.

The golden age of Buddhism in Japan extended from the twelfth through the sixteenth centuries. During this time a Buddhist fervor for immediate salvation spread throughout all classes and permeated all aspects of Japanese culture. The Buddhist church had also become rich as a landowner and often exercised considerable temporal power. In 1175 a priest known as Hōnen founded the Jōdo sect, based on the concept of immediate salvation through faith in the "Pure Land" paradise of Amida. In 1224 Shinran founded a reformed variant of this sect, later known as the Jōdo-Shin, which was to become numerically the largest of all Japanese denominations. In 1252 Nichiren founded the Lotus sect, based on the worship of the *Lotus Sutra*, rather than Amida. Intolerant of other sects and iconoclastic in his views, Nichiren was continually in conflict with the government and the other branches of Buddhism, but his sect, which came to be known by his name, prospered.

Meanwhile monks recently returned from study in China founded in 1191 and 1227 the two main lines of the Zen sect. The warrior class, which rose to the fore as feudalism took hold in Japan between the twelfth and the fourteenth centuries, came to develop a special affinity for the strong self-discipline of Zen. Zen masters and the ideas and artistic achievements of the sect became the dominant cultural influences of the fourteenth to sixteenth centuries.

Following a long period of feudal division and warfare, Japan was reunited by military force at the beginning of the seventeenth century. During the resulting period of peace and stability, Confucian doctrines came to be emphasized in Japan, and Buddhism, as it had five or six centuries earlier in China, began a long, slow decline both in intellectual vigor and in popularity. At the same time, however, the whole population of Japan was forced to enroll in local Buddhist parishes, in part to enforce anti-Christian decrees. This situation continued until the second half of the nineteenth century, and as a result the Japanese remain today in large part titular Buddhists.

Most Japanese are in theory both Buddhists and Shintoists. This may seem strange to Westerners, Middle Easterners, and south Asians, who are accustomed to the fierce exclusiveness of their own religions. In early Japan the mutual toleration of Buddhism and Shinto was probably made possible because the two were so different. Each addressed itself to different aspects of Japanese life and religious feelings. Shinto was concerned with the wonders of nature and the cycle of everyday life, paying scant heed to grand philosophical ideas or even matters involving the afterlife. Buddhism was obsessed with escape from a painful chain of after lives and the achievement of immediate salvation. It offered satisfying rituals to honor deceased ancestors. It delighted in philosophical hair-splitting. Buddhism had a sophisticated literature and gorgeously developed art, both of which Shinto lacked. Buddhism and Shinto, in fact, overlapped very little. Each fitted into its own ecological niche in Japanese life. After only a brief initial clash over rival claims to magical powers, they quickly settled down to a peaceful and harmonious coexistence.

Living side by side over the centuries, Buddhism and Shinto began to coalesce and merge. Their temples and shrines often became joint institutions. Shinto deities were conceived of as the local Japanese manifestation of more universal Buddhist spiritual forces. The very parochial nationalism of the one kept it from clashing with the universal, cosmic nature of the other. But bit by bit each lost some of its distinctiveness, until many folk beliefs and practices could no longer be identified as being clearly Shinto or Buddhist but shared characteristics of both.

A reassertion of Shinto individuality, started in the late eighteenth century, and a harsh government policy, following the Meiji Restoration of 1868, enforced the institutional divorce of Shinto and Buddhist organizations, clearly establishing the distinction between the two religions in modern times. The characteristic Shinto *torii* gateway and basically dissimilar forms of architecture help make the division visually apparent. It has also become an accepted practice in English to call all Shinto holy places "shrines" and all Buddhist ones "temples," unless the activities associated with the Buddhist "temple" make the term "monastery" more suitable. But as Professor Picken's text makes clear, for the ordinary Japanese the lines between Buddhism and Shinto remain quite blurred in actual religious practice.

Most works on Japanese Buddhism are overwhelmed by the long, complex history of the religion, the extraordinary diversity and subtlety of its philosophy, or the richness of its art and literature. Such matters Professor Picken has passed over lightly, concentrating instead on Buddhism as part of the religious life of the average Japanese. It is here we see how Buddhism first found a distinctive place for itself in Japanese culture and then gradually merged with the other religious feelings of the Japanese to form an almost seamless continuum with Shinto. The peaceful, harmonious blending of Buddhism and Shinto in Japan provide a happy contrast to the harsh conflict of religions in some other parts of the world.

Edwin O. Reischauer

1 Origins and the Eastward Flow

I take refuge in the Buddha;
I take refuge in the Buddhist Law;
I take refuge in the Buddhist Community.

the Buddhist confession of faith

Land of Seventy-Thousand Temples

It may be hard for Westerners to associate Buddhism with Japan. Buddhism suggests the exotic and the mysterious; it conjures up images of incense-filled temples, chanting and rituals, lotus buds and statues of Buddhas. Japan, on the other hand, is the land of the technological miracle, the land of robot-built automobiles and digital electronics. But, just as traditional religion and modern industrial civilization have found ways to coexist in the West, so too they have managed to do in Japan. Japan the economic superpower is still the land of a hundred-thousand Shinto shrines and seventy-thousand Buddhist temples.

While Buddhism in Japan does indeed possess mysterious elements, it also has a work-a-day face and a long tradition of involvement in the daily lives of ordinary people, to the extent that it has become a practical religion of the people, one manner of expressing the native Japanese spirituality, seen in its purest form in Shinto. In addition, it has taken on the role of guarantor of social continuity and of the unity and cultural identity of the Japanese people. Buddhism in Japan has become Japanese Buddhism to a degree that makes it difficult to distinguish the two terms. Japan has transformed Buddhism to meet its own needs and yet, at the same time, has tried to be faithful in its own ways to the insights of the founder. It is to these insights that we must first turn in order to appreciate the unique way in which the Japanese mind adapted Buddhism to articulate some of the deepest longings of the Japanese spirit, a process of adaptation that took some six centuries to reach fruition.

The Foundations of Buddhism

Buddhism originated in India and grew to become the great missionary religion of the East, although nowadays in the land of its birth it claims the adherence of only some three to four percent of the population. Buddhism is practiced in a form closest to its original precepts—with strict observance of the monastic rules—in Sri Lanka, Burma, and Thailand. Saffron-robed monks are a familiar sight in these countries, and women can be seen avoiding physical contact with them on crowded buses or along busy thoroughfares. This is the simple Buddhism of the monastery, where ordination means, not years of academic training leading to ecclesiastical approval as with Christianity, but the honest desire to follow the path of the Buddha according to the Four Noble Truths and the Eightfold Path, which he first enunciated and taught. These ideas may be stated in the form of intellectual propositions, but in essence they are a means of guidance for us so that we can live our lives according to the principles of gentleness, reverence for life, and profound self-reflection.

THE FOUR NOBLE TRUTHS

1. All existence involves suffering.
2. The cause of suffering is desire, because desire leads to rebirth.
3. The cessation of suffering can only be achieved through the cessation of desire.
4. The way of the Eightfold Path ends desire.

A World of Suffering

The idea that all forms of existence are permeated by suffering was the original, fundamental truth perceived in the sixth century B.C. by Siddartha Gautama, the son of a leading citizen of Kapilavastu, a city lying in the northeast corner of the Indian subcontinent in what is now the country of Nepal. Shocked by the sight of suffering, old age, disease, and death and dissatisfied with the conventional religion of sacrificial Brahmanism and the excessive austerity of the Jainists, he "awoke" to the true condition of mankind and started preaching the Middle Way between worldly concerns and extreme asceticism.

Not all the ideas of Buddha ("the Enlightened One") were the fruits of his own insight. He shared two concepts found throughout the religious thought of the Indian subcontinent: *samsara*, the endless cycle of birth, death, and rebirth; and *karma*, the inexorable moral law that dictates our fate in the cycle of birth and rebirth. These doctrines are the product of a deeply pessimistic outlook; improvement—rebirth in a higher status—while not impossible, is very difficult and may take thousands of lifetimes to accomplish. The Buddha himself had six hundred previous lives, during which he had struggled to find understanding; others may well take longer. *Karma* is sometimes presented as analogous to the idea of sin in the Christian tradition. This, however, is not a helpful comparison. Whereas accumulated good *karma* may give hope for a better reincarnation, accumulated bad *karma* cannot be forgiven; it can only be expiated by rebirth. The hunter who shoots a bird may be reborn as a bird and, in turn, be caught, killed, and eaten.

The Buddha taught the way to release from the cycle of birth and rebirth. His way—awareness of the Four Noble Truths and a life conducted in accordance with the Eightfold Path—is the way to liberation from this cycle and to the state of nirvana, the final stage of release from *karma* and *samsara*.

THE EIGHTFOLD PATH

1. Right outlook: to know the Four Noble Truths.
2. Right resolve: to overcome illusions caused by belief in an individual self.
3. Right speech: to refrain from untruth and frivolity.
4. Right conduct: to avoid harming living beings and to relieve suffering.
5. Right livelihood: to have an occupation in keeping with Buddhist precepts.
6. Right effort: to show determination to reach salvation.
7. Right mindfulness: to realize the dangers of discontents that arise from various physical and mental states.
8. Right concentration: to be free of distractions and illusions and to be alert and reflective.

Of the eight, the first two and the last two refer to achieving a state of mind and the middle four to the correct conduct of one's life. The fourth principle, that of nonviolence, has proved particularly attractive to many who have come into contact with Buddhism, and it remains one of Buddhism's identifying features. The high moral tone of the Eightfold Path puts it on a par with the Ten Commandments of Moses and Jesus' Sermon on the Mount.

The Small and the Great Vehicles

In its early stages, Buddhism was entirely monastic and male, and in many countries where it is still the dominant faith, it continues to be a religion of the monastery. A person becoming a monk—seven is the minimum age—takes a threefold vow: to seek refuge in the Buddha (as teacher), the *dharma* (law), and the *sangha* (community). His head is shaved, and he receives a begging bowl as the source of his livelihood. He may spend the rest of his life in a monk's robe, or, more likely, he may plan to return to the secular life within as little as six months or a year. Whichever is the case, his life in the monastery will be one of frugality and moderation: only one meal a day, but fasting is prohibited. The smoking of cigarettes is not forbidden, nor is the use of sunglasses. The purpose remains to create a lifestyle that enables people to live simply and to understand themselves better. Consequently, extreme rigors are discouraged.

This is the type of Buddhism that is closest to the original intentions of the religion's founder. It is usually called Theravada, which means the "way of the elders," but is also known as Hinayana, the "small vehicle." This latter name was given it by believers in Mahayana, the "great vehicle," a later development of Buddhism that first flourished in northwest India and was eventually transmitted to Japan via Central Asia, China, and Korea. Mahayana is a general

A monk meets villagers in the countryside of Sri Lanka, a nation adhering to Hinayana Buddhism.

name used to identify a wide grouping of alternative interpretations of Buddhism, interpretations that differ in their understanding of the Four Noble Truths and in how the Eightfold Path should be followed. Mahayana claims that its scriptures (sutras), which are written in Sanskrit, represent the true message of the historical Buddha.

The origins of Mahayana Buddhism can be traced back to the philosopher Ashvaghosha, who lived in India sometime around the second century A.D. and who wrote the *Awakening of Faith in the Mahayana Doctrine*, a text which exists no longer in the original Sanskrit but only in a Chinese translation. In it he argued that after the Buddha had entered nirvana few people really understood the possibilities inherent in his teachings. Ashvaghosha then proceeded to expound some of these possibilities by translating Buddhism into the categories of Indian metaphysics.

Out of this emerged a series of schools of thought which agreed that the role of the bodhisattva as an intermediary communicator of truth was central to Buddhist teaching. Armed with his knowledge of the truth, a bodhisattva delays his entry into nirvana in order to assist us unenlightened human beings, who are the victims of our own ignorance. We are unable to see things as they really are, and so we wrestle futilely with illusion. Nagarjuna, who is thought to have lived in the second or third century A.D. and is often considered the greatest philosopher of Mahayana Buddhism, illustrated the point in his parable of the monk with diseased eyes, who was sitting by the roadside begging and flailing the air with his hands. The Buddha passed by and asked him why he was waving. "To shoo away the flies in my begging bowl," he answered. We are like the monk, Nagarjuna tells us, in our insistence in regarding as real what we see through our distorted perception. The Mahayana version of Buddhism is an attempt to expose human illusion and to cultivate a deeper awareness of the reality that lies behind it.

Buddhism in China

If the elaboration of Mahayana doctrines was one stage in Buddhism's long journey to Japan, another stage consisted of its intercourse with Chinese civilization. In China it underwent a long process of cultural transformation as a result of contact with the long-established traditions of a sophisticated civilization entirely different from that prevalent in the Indian subcontinent.

When Buddhism made its appearance in China in the first few centuries A.D., introduced by merchants and monks from central Asia and northwest India, a massive amount of work had to be done to translate the voluminous Mahayana canon of sutras and shastras, commentaries on the sutras. Translation between two languages as syntactically different as Sanskrit and Chinese involved great linguistic and conceptual problems—for example, how to express in Chinese ideas for which there were no Chinese equivalents. The answer, as often as not, was to use Taoist terms and to resort to considerable freedom of expression. The result of all this was that Buddhism in China developed independently of the controversies and metaphysics of India. The process has been described as one in which the Chinese asked the questions and merely used Indian Buddhist revelation to supply the answers.

Mahayana Buddhism, for its part, showed considerable flexibility in making adjustments to Chinese culture as well as a willingness to mix with local cults. Of all the features of Chinese civilization with which it had to come to terms, one of the most deep-rooted—in China as in Japan—was the exalted position occupied by the family ancestors. Buddhism's readiness to accommodate itself to this attitude of reverence for ancestors was a decisive factor in its acceptance by both the Chinese and the Japanese.

A form of Tantric Buddhism, derived from the Mahayana tradition, spread to Tibet, and—as these unusual photograhs, taken in the streets of Lhasa, show—it is still the object of devotion.

The 13.5-meter-high Colossal Buddha at Yungang in Shanxi Province, north China, dates from the fifth century.

Buddhism's penetration of Chinese civilization was not, however, easily accomplished. In the fifth century A.D., about a hundred years before its existence in Japan was officially recognized, Buddhism was the target of persecution in the north of China and of polemical attacks in the south. One Buddhist response to criticism came in the form of a treatise, probably written about this time, entitled *The Settling of Doubts*, the aim of which was to show that Buddhism was not incompatible with the traditional Chinese pattern of life. For example, when it is asked why Buddhism is not mentioned in the Chinese classics, the author of the treatise argues that as long as Buddhism is not inconsistent with the classics and providing it promotes social well-being, then it must be good, in which case Confucius would have approved of it.

The Chinese reacted sensitively to certain Buddhist practices such as shaving the head and celibacy for the clergy. The former involved "injuring" the human body, which was a gift from one's parents. The latter made fulfilment of true filial piety impossible, since the duties to one's parents were realized in the perpetuation of the family through the birth of children. Similarly, the idea of reincarnation created anxiety about the state of ancestral spirits, who were believed to be unhappy if not fed. Questions were also asked about the legitimacy of permitting Chinese civilization to be influenced by alien ways. *The Settling of Doubts* thus indicates which points of Buddhist doctrine were modified through reinterpretation before they were fully accepted, and, while no such document exists in Japan, it is interesting nonetheless for students of Japanese Buddhism in that it shows how problematical points were anticipated and circumvented in China and thus made easier to accept in Japan.

Buddhism in China had encountered a civilization of great sophistication with its own anthropocentric philosophy, whose basic premises were at odds with those of Buddhism. It had, however, managed to adapt itself, and in time had come to be regarded as one of the three great "ways" of China, alongside Confucianism and Taoism. It held this position of eminence for several centuries until the beginning of its decline as a powerful, organized force in China, which came about as a result of sustained persecution in the ninth and tenth centuries.

When the Japanese were introduced to it, Buddhism was no longer—as it had been for the Chinese—an Indian cult transmitted by itinerant monks and scholars but the bearer of Chinese civilization itself. It was the virtual indistinguishability of the two, the civilization and the religion, that helped facilitate the absorption of Buddhism into the Japanese mind and soul, where it mingled with the indigenous cults and produced the various movements that have vitalized the history of Japanese religion. The spiritual roots of Japanese civilization are to be found in the rituals and ideals of Shinto, but its cultural identity is deeply permeated by Buddhism.

1. Fallen cherry blossoms floating on the water (*right*) are a reminder of the fundamental Buddhist truth that perfection is unattainable because life is transient and all things are in an endless state of flux. Similarly, happiness and sorrow, love and suffering are states of mind that ebb and flow, and the wise man tries to detach himself from them by seeking enlightenment.

2. This ancient *bodhi* tree (*preceding photograph*) stands near the site where the historical Buddha is believed to have gained enlightenment. It was under a *bodhi* tree (a species of fig tree native to the Indian subcontinent) that the Buddha sat meditating, until he found the perfect release of enlightenment and the law of emancipation, which he distilled into the Four Noble Truths. Statues of the Buddha most frequently represent him meditating in the seated position he assumed under the *bodhi* tree. Here, in these symbols of faith, is a basic contrast between Buddhism and Christianity: the pose of enlightenment and the suffering on the cross, the lotus and the crown of thorns.

3. The construction of this colossal bronze statue (*left*) of the Rushana Buddha, known as the Nara *daibutsu,* was begun in 745 at the Tōdai-ji in Nara. Work on the statue took many years, and there were times when difficulties both technical and financial appeared unsurmountable. Eventually, as a result of the labors of, it is said, over eight thousand artists and craftsmen and the discovery of gold in Japan (the very best of good omens), the statue was completed. It stands sixteen meters high under the roof of the largest wooden building in the world (although the original building, which was even larger than the present one, was destroyed and the statue seriously damaged in the civil warfare of the twelfth century). The ceremony to "open the Buddha's eyes" was held in the spring of 752 in the presence of the emperor Shōmu, one of the most pious and enthusiastic imperial patrons of Buddhism. The head and much of the body of the Nara *daibutsu* date from the late seventeenth century.

4. One of the most familiar sights at temples is that of worshipers lighting incense and then drawing the fumes over their bodies for protection or for treatment of physical and spiritual ailments. The incense burner in this photograph is an unusually big one hewn out of a rock in a temple near the town of Tsukiyono in Gumma Prefecture in the mountains north of Tokyo. In fact, this is no ordinary place of worship but a mortuary temple built on the spot where Sugiki Mozaemon, a peasant hero, was crucified in the 1680s, his penalty for having been successful, through the use of a cunning ruse, in ousting a local lord whose rule had been characterized by uncommon cruelty.

5. Autumn leaves (*overleaf*) beckon an elderly couple into the grounds of a temple in the town of Asuke near Nagoya. Like the main square of a Mediterranean town, temple grounds often come to be social gathering points, not only for older people but also for mothers who want some space for their children to play around in, or indeed for anyone passing by. In busy Japanese cities the grounds of a temple are often the best place to sit down and take a rest.

2 The Japanese Transformation of Buddhism

If any king upholds this sutra, . . . I will protect his cities,
towns and villages, and scatter his enemies.

Sutra of the Golden Light

All human beings have the lotus of buddhahood within them.

Saichō, founder of the Tendai sect

Buddhism's Outposts

Buddhism grew out of the tradition of Indian religious thought, but it was in other parts of Asia that it enjoyed its greatest success. It is more in evidence in contemporary Japan than it is in India, where it reached the summit of its influence in the third century B.C. under the patronage of the emperor Ashoka.

Although the analogy should not be drawn too far, Buddhism seems to have attracted Ashoka in much the same way that Christianity attracted the Roman emperor Constantine, who was largely responsible for the state recognition of Christianity within the Roman Empire. In spite of having been a military leader, Ashoka embraced Buddhist precepts, issued a series of edicts enjoining Buddhist ideals on his subjects, and dispatched envoys to various parts of Asia and even to the Mediterranean. During his reign, the Third Buddhist Council was held at Patna on the banks of the Ganges. It was from there that the great missionary wave emerged, and it was there too that the cleavage of opinion sharpened, resulting in the beginnings of the conscious separation of Hinayana and Mahayana teachings about the nature of Buddhist truth. The island of Sri Lanka, where the entire canon of Hinayana Buddhist literature (written in the Pali language) is preserved, was evangelized according to legend by Ashoka's son and daughter. Japan, almost at the opposite end of Asia, remains one of the finest examples of a civilization deeply influenced not by Hinayana but by the other great strain of Buddhism, Mahayana—a civilization which interacted with Buddhism in a manner made possible by Mahayana's flexibility. After Buddhism had begun to decline in the land of its birth, these outposts ensured its survival.

The acceptance of Buddhism by Asian civilizations such as that of Japan was a gradual process. The Japanese did not become converted to Buddhism as one race, nor, on the whole, did individual Japanese make a conscious decision to become Buddhist. The acceptance of Buddhism involved a slow transformation of culture, with the Buddhist ideas that had been transplanted onto Japanese soil being allowed to bear their own type of fruit in the fullness of time. In Japan, as in other lands into which Buddhism flowed, a rich civilization began to emerge based on a meeting between what Buddhism had to offer the Japanese and what the Japanese saw in Buddhist culture as being useful to their purpose. Japan, however, did not become —as did Sri Lanka and Thailand, for example—a Buddhist civilization under a Buddhist government. It became a civilization bearing the indelible imprint of Buddhist culture.

Shōtoku Taishi

The successful spread of Buddhism depended not only on the efforts of wandering teachers and evangelists but also on the patronage of the nobility of the many countries through which it flowed. Various were the rulers it appealed to, and various too were the reasons it appealed to them. In Japan Buddhism attracted the support of Shōtoku Taishi (574–622), prince regent to his aunt the empress Suiko, because of its role as the bearer of a civilization. Prince Shōtoku was the first great promulgator of Buddhism in Japan. He promoted Buddhism both on grounds of personal belief and because he was impressed by the religion as part of a higher civilization.

The years of Shōtoku Taishi's rule saw a number of humanitarian reforms instituted, reforms that marked an important stage in the development of Japanese civilization. The prince had sent a series of missions to China, and it was partly as a result of the impressions they received of the splendor of Chinese civilization that Shōtoku decided to model his transformation of Japan along Chinese lines, with pride of place given to Buddhism and to Confucian teaching, which in China provided the basis of an intricate social system founded on the principles of harmony and filial piety. The combined influence of Buddhism and Confucianism can be seen in the set of moral guidelines enunciated by Shōtoku Taishi in the year 604 in the form of Seventeen Articles. The first of the Seventeen Articles stresses harmony as the fundamental principle of society, whereas the second article suggests that the realization of this principle depends on reverence for the Three Buddhist

6. The Yakushi-ji, one of the most magnificent of the temples of Nara, was founded in the seventh century and moved to its present site in the eighth. The pagodas have three tiers, unlike most Japanese pagodas, which have five. But because of their design they are the same height as a five-tiered pagoda. The Yakushi-ji, like other temples in Nara, was built in the Chinese style. In later centuries, temple buildings came to incorporate certain architectural features, like thatched roofs and raised wooden floors, not found in China, features that represent a native integration into architectural style of the Japanese feeling for harmony with nature.

7. In the Chūgū-ji, a nunnery attached to the Hōryū-ji, sits this statue of the bodhisattva Miroku (*right*), carved in camphorwood and bearing the traces of coloring. It dates from around the middle of the seventh century and is one of the most famous of several sculptural representations of Miroku in this classic pose of meditation. The image carries many signs of the influence of Chinese styles of the preceding century, and it is not hard to imagine that, with its benign smile and its profound composure, this figure and others like it proved an irresistible attraction and a powerful advertisement for the newly arrived religion.

Treasures: the Buddha, the Law, and the Community. He also taught in a simple way that the wrongs of everyday life could be corrected by observance of the Buddhist law.

Buddhist influences had in fact already been filtering into Japan, introduced by migrants from China and Korea, well before the time of Shōtoku Taishi. This process reached a sort of culmination with the presentation in 552 of some Buddhist images and sutras to the imperial court by Japan's Korean ally, the king of Paekche, an event that marked formal recognition of the new religion by the court and ushered in a new stage in the development of Buddhism in Japan.

It was, however, due to the efforts of Shōtoku Taishi that Buddhism began to acquire a formal identity as part of Japanese culture. He promoted the building of several important monasteries and temples, and he was personally responsible for the erection of the Shitennō-ji (temple of the four heavenly kings) in Osaka in 593 as well as the temple, monastery, and seminary complex of the Hōryū-ji in Nara in 607. By the time of his death, over forty temples had been built, and Buddhism had acquired a physical presence in the country.

Buddhism, the State, and Protection
The Nara period (711–93) saw the gradual Buddhist ecclesiastification of Japanese culture and the emergence of a form of government which regarded Buddhism as a protective agency. As early as the year 660, there is a reference to a meeting held by order of the empress to hear an exposition of the *Sutra of the Benevolent King*. Out of this grew the custom of an annual lecture in the imperial palace on the subject of this sutra, and the belief arose that the sutra was in itself a form of protection of the state. It was read to consecrate and bless the newly established capital of Kyoto in 794, and it retained its prominent position among the sutras until about the thirteenth century.

The chanting of sutras was widely practiced as a form of protection for the state and the people. But it was more than just a question of sutras; the nation's political leaders seem to have promoted Buddhism quite consciously for the sake of the preservation of the state rather than from concern for the salvation of individual souls. This does not mean that their view of religion was a cynical one. Religion was understood primarily in terms of its collective benefits to society rather than in terms of its contribution to the spiritual well-being of individuals. If religion worked for the well-being of the whole of society, then individuals would benefit from a sound moral and spiritual environment. To Buddhism may be attributed the development in Japan of the principle that it is the task of government to promote collective well-being and thus ensure individual security.

The idea of protection also won for Buddhism its acceptance among the mass of ordinary people, for whom Buddhist deities were simply foreign versions of the native Shinto *kami*, or divine beings, and thus possessed the same powers as the *kami* to protect them from illness and disasters. Agriculture was a special area of concern; the first sutras to be introduced into Japan were chanted in order to bring weather propitious to the healthy growth and abundant harvesting of rice. The essence of ancient Buddhism was the performance of rituals and ceremonies (a feature that has continued down to the present day), but it does not seem to have been a matter of great concern for the ordinary people to distinguish between ceremonies directed to Buddhist divinities and those to the native *kami*. Although separate government departments supervised Shinto shrines and Buddhist temples, the popular imagination seems not to have drawn such a clear line. Moreover, with the development over the centuries of the numerous schools and sects and with their transformation into a purely Japanese mold, relations between Shinto and Buddhism became more complex.

The Development of the Sects
Japanese Buddhism is divided into "sects" or "schools" (*shū*), some of which were consciously founded, while others evolved out of older sects. Every temple belongs to one or another of the sects. It is generally said that there are twelve Buddhist sects in Japan, half of which were founded in the Nara period. Of these six—the Jōjitsu, Kusha, Hossō, Sanron, Ritsu, and Kegon sects—some no

The Hōryū-ji in Nara, which contains the oldest wooden buildings in the world, is laid out in the manner of Chinese temples.

longer even exist in an organized form. All of them, however, played their part in the development of Japanese Buddhism, and the Kegon sect—with its headquarters in Nara, the Tōdai-ji, a sort of national cathedral—is one that has continued to survive.

During the Heian period (794–1184) two schools of esoteric Buddhism, the Tendai and the Shingon, were introduced from China. These sects (they are discussed in detail in chapter nine) combined with the native cults of Shinto to produce a hybrid set of practices known as *shugendō*, a distinctive type of mountain religion that combined esoteric Buddhism and mountain asceticism. The last four in the traditionally accepted list of twelve Buddhist sects are the four great movements originating in the Kamakura period (1185–1332), which were to have such a lasting influence on the nature of Japanese Buddhism. Of the four, Zen is the exception in that it is largely contemplative, while the other three are, broadly speaking, popular and devotional. These are the two Pure Land sects, the Jōdo and the Jōdo-Shin, and the sect formed by the followers of Nichiren, the most colorful personality of those tempestuous centuries.

Of the great number of Mahayana sutras (*kyō* in Japanese), some grew fashionable for a period and then lapsed into relative obscurity; among these are the *Sutra of the Benevolent King*, which we have already mentioned in connection with protection of the state, and the *Flower Wreath (Kegon) Sutra*, which is closely connected with the Kegon sect of the Nara period. Others, however, have remained popular. The perennial favorite is the *Lotus Sutra*, which has inspired new developments in Japanese Buddhism starting from the early ninth century and the Tendai school through the thirteenth century and Nichiren to the postwar period, when Buddhism has been almost entirely devoted to the *Lotus Sutra*.

The Simplification of Buddhism in Japan

> Have no further doubts;
> Rejoice greatly in your hearts,
> Knowing that you will become Buddhas.

Little could express better than these lines from the *Lotus Sutra* the spirit of Japanese Buddhism; for of the various ways in which Buddhism changed its nature in Japan through the centuries, one of the most characteristic was the tendency to simplify its central doctrines and to focus on the ideal of attaining buddhahood in one lifetime.

In the Buddhism of India, the attainment of buddhahood, or enlightenment, called for an almost superhuman degree of effort and determination. Few people were capable of exerting such effort, and therefore enlightenment was in reality almost unattainable. Japanese Buddhism, on the other hand, teaches that buddhahood can be attained while one is alive or at the latest immediately after death. This theme became an established part of the funeral liturgies of all the sects. The esoteric tradition of Shingon and Tendai, related to the Tantric schools of Tibet, teaches the

This unique twelfth-century copy of the *Lotus Sutra* is inscribed on fan-shaped leaves illustrated with scenes from everyday life.

Every temple has its bell. This one is in the grounds of the Kiyosumi-dera in Chiba Prefecture, east of Tokyo.

principle of enlightenment in the physical body, while the Pure Land Buddhism of the Jōdo and Jōdo-Shin sects holds out the promise of rebirth in the Western Paradise of Amida. Zen takes meditation as a means to instantaneous enlightenment, whereas for the followers of Nichiren the chanting of the name of the *Lotus Sutra* is itself sufficient.

Closely related to this is a second distinctive feature of the sort of Buddhism that developed in Japan—namely, the role of the bodhisattva as an intermediary between those seeking buddhahood and those who have already attained it, a role similar to that otherwise filled by the clergy. Priests just as much as laypeople seek enlightenment, and, since devotion toward and identification with a favorite bodhisattva is one means of approaching buddhahood, it is not surprising that a feature of Japanese Buddhism was the gradual lessening of the distinction between priest and layperson. While for practical purposes of temple administration the distinction continues, the gap in styles of living and daily behavior has closed to the point where a priest on business involving nonceremonial duties might easily be taken for a businessman commuting to his office. Some of the modern Buddhist movements—for example, Risshō Kōsei-kai—style themselves movements of Buddhist laypeople and stress that both priests and laity have the right to take the initiative in developing and expressing new ideas. Since 1868, all the sects have followed the lead of Jōdo-Shin in allowing their priests to marry. Women are also "permitted" to attain buddhahood, and they have their place too in the workings of Buddhist organizations.

The ideal of the bodhisattva—to show compassion in all aspects of daily life—is an ideal taught by all branches of Japanese Buddhism. Priests and laypeople alike must learn to show the compassion of a bodhisattva if they hope to attain buddhahood.

A third distinctive characteristic of Buddhism in Japan in some way embraces these two features: the consistent tendency to stress the spirit rather than the letter of Buddhist law, so that Buddhist law can be modified to meet the changing needs of the times. This is the crux of the Japanese view of the name Mahayana, the "great vehicle," which for them is great enough to change its form so as to better express the spirit of the Buddha in a world vastly different from that in which Buddhism had its beginnings. The Buddhist prohibition about eating meat, for example, was observed in Japan in a way which left a clear imprint on Japanese eating habits—hence their liking for vegetables and seaweed—but which seldom prevented them from enjoying fish and the occasional dish of meat. Buddhism is not being ignored; it is being flexibly interpreted.

There are still those in Buddhism, as there are those within the Christian tradition, who equate the existence of the true faith with preservation of the structures of past society. According to this definition, it can be argued that modern Japanese Buddhism is not Buddhism at all. However, it is the essence of Japanese Buddhism that it is changeable, and this is what makes the new movements discussed in chapter ten as much bearers of the Buddhist tradition in Japan as the great sects with a long history like the Pure Land sects and Zen.

3 Traditional Buddhism in Modern Society

At the edge of the village
He stands, smiling
Ever smiling—Jizō.
See there, how he watches!

children's song

Omamori—Buddhist Talismans

Buddhism's traditional protective role is a good point at which to start an examination of the part Buddhism plays in contemporary Japan (leaving the funeral—its biggest contribution—to the next chapter). Visit any temple in Japan and, as likely as not, you will see on display in the temple precincts an apparently endless number of good-luck charms, amulets, and talismans for believers to take with them on journeys, to carry for success in examinations or in business, or to help in recovery from an illness. They are known as *omamori*, a term that comes from the Japanese word *mamoru*, meaning to "protect" or "defend." In ancient times *omamori* were probably carried in small bags, and in fact they are still often contained in little pouches bearing the name of the temple and the purpose of the *omamori*.

The origins of the practice of carrying *omamori* are to be found in Shinto rather than in Buddhism, Shinto having grown out of a long tradition of folk religion. Shinto recognized the *kami*, or divine, nature of things and tried to harness this power for protection and strength. Buddhism for its part absorbed this tradition, just as religions everywhere learn to pay respect to folk customs, whether these are in the form of Saint Christopher medallions or other adapted relics of some ancient belief like the rabbit's foot or the four-leaf clover, not to mention Santa Claus and Easter eggs.

The Japanese often insist that they are neither very religious nor very superstitious, but the sheer extensiveness of the practice of carrying *omamori* suggests a profoundly felt dependence upon a power beyond themselves and the belief that, if they carry something of the power of a great being with them, protection and security will result. Many *omamori*, but by no means all, are meant to be carried on the body—hanging from belts, handbags, key rings, or pockets. Others are designed to protect the home or the family automobile, the shop, or the office, indeed almost anything that can be protected.

Sitting in a barbershop one day, I was flicking over the pages of a weekly magazine of a kind that normally spe-cializes in sex and scandals when I found a fascinating example of how Buddhism adapts to the ways of the modern world in order to offer its protective powers. Work had just been completed at the Dai Kannon-ji, a temple in Mie Prefecture south of Nagoya, on a vast new image of Kannon, and the temple authorities were offering for sale medallions that had been minted to mark the occasion. These medallions were both congratulatory and protective in nature. The idea was to get members of the public to buy a medallion with the symbol appropriate to the year of his birth in the twelve-year cycle of the oriental zodiac.

Three points struck me about the advertisement. The first was that as a full-page advertisement it would have cost a substantial sum of money, and so the temple authorities must have expected to sell a fair number of medallions. Secondly, they clearly considered the readers of that magazine as potential customers. Thirdly, the prices started from five hundred dollars per medallion! It would be hard to imagine Madison Avenue Presbyterian Church advertising services or Saint Patrick's Cathedral offering mail-order Saint Christophers in a girlie magazine. Here was revealing testimony of how close Buddhism lies to the hearts of ordinary people in Japan.

The *shōfuku-temi*, "rice scoop (symbolizing prosperity) of good fortune," is an agglomeration of *omamori*. The five-yen coin involves a pun on "*go*," which means "five" and "*karma*," and "*en*," the process of causation. The bell is an ancient symbol of exorcism.

In most larger temples there is a counter or a separate building where a priest sits selling *omamori* like those shown above to be hung, for example, in a car or truck.

Protection in Danger, Illness, and Death

Travel is a department of life which, fraught as it is with dangers, has always involved a need for protection. The mercy of the bodhisattva Kannon is often directed toward road safety, and statues of Kannon can be found housed in small canopied shrines alongside highways, put there either by the local authorities or by local residents to protect users of the road against accidents. Health too is an area in which divine protective powers are often called on, Buddhas and bodhisattvas having been popular since ancient times as guardians of health and curers of disease. Many temples contain Buddhist images that are regarded as having curative powers, and it is not uncommon, even in these days of sophisticated medical treatment, for people to visit a temple well known for being efficacious in the cure of a certain ailment. Thus a young couple whose child has a persistent cough that medicines appear unable to cure might visit one temple, while a woman in her sixties with rheumatism might see if a visit to another temple has any effect in relieving her pain.

Death calls for protection of a slightly different sort, and here the popular bodhisattva Jizō plays a preeminent role. Jizō continues in the twentieth century, as he did in the past, to oversee the welfare of the souls of dead babies and of babies who never saw the light of day. There are temples throughout Japan with statues of Jizō at which parents offer prayers for their dead children or aborted fetuses (pl. 8). One of these, the Shōjo-in, a temple in Kita Ward in the north of Tokyo, enshrined a statue of Jizō in 1951. According to data supplied by the temple, up to one hundred women a day come to pray at the temple for their dead babies, aborted fetuses, or stillborn children. As a form of therapy, women are encouraged to write down their experiences and feelings, some of which are moving in their honesty:

> —I was gifted with a small life in my body, but it was too early for me and my husband....I feel sorry for my baby.
> —Today I am here to say that I feel sorry and that I feel relieved of my burden by this prayer.

Some, however, are not so easily assuaged:

> —I feel a deep wrong within me, and I regret I could not be with you. I pray that your soul will become a good Buddha beside Jizō-san.

Occasionally fathers too leave a note. One father had written the following message:

> —My baby, please forgive this helpless father. May your soul rest in peace. Your foolish father.

The temple image of Jizō is usually surrounded by toys, dolls, feeding bottles, candies—apologies for not having observed the principle of reverence for life. The spirit of Buddhism lives on in attitudes such as this.

The Buddhist Calendar

A visit to a temple to pray for help and protection might take place at any time of year. There are, however, certain fixed occasions during the year when the temple grounds are filled with worshipers. The most important of these occasions is the New Year. At least eighty million people —three-quarters of the population of the whole country— pay a visit to a shrine or temple in the first few days of the new year, a visit that is known as *hatsumōde*. Celebrating the New Year was originally a Shinto custom, and the majority of people still visit Shinto shrines. Nevertheless, New Year has become a Buddhist festival too, and lots of people visit temples, especially those belonging to the Tendai and Shingon sects, many of which once had a close connection with Shinto.

Buddhism has another connection with the New Year celebrations, a ritual unique to Japanese Buddhism known as *joya no kane*. As midnight approaches on New Year's Eve, temple bells are rung 108 times—symbolizing the 108 forms of defilement—to mark the end of the old year. NHK, Japan's national broadcasting corporation, never fails to take its cameras up to a mountain temple on New Year's Eve. Punctuating the usual scenes of celebration from various parts of the country, the picture returns from time to time to the temple as the bell is struck. At the very moment of midnight, the cameras show the temple priest pulling at a long rope, and so, through the seasonal sentimentality and merrymaking of the television shows, the boom of a Buddhist bell ushers in the new year.

Several of the other annual ceremonies which are connected with Buddhism involve rites for the dead (see chapter five). Two important dates in the Buddhist calendar are 21 March and 23 September, public holidays to mark the spring and autumn equinox, when families traditionally visit the ancestral grave. *Obon*, the Japanese All Souls' Day, is another festival with Buddhist connections, celebrated normally in July or August. The birthday of the historical Buddha, known as *hanamatsuri*, the "flower festival," is marked on 8 April (pl. 9). The Buddha's death (or, to be precise, his entry into nirvana) is commemorated on 15 February. Buddhism has a thanksgiving day as well, in the summer, when temple parishioners gather at the temple to offer thanks for the blessings they have received.

The Different Types of Temple

The temple is the central institution of Buddhism in Japan. It is there that all the ceremonies take place, priests live and work, and most of the important events of the Buddhist calendar are marked—there and at the family grave. Every old temple is a place with its own fascinating history (even if the buildings themselves are modern, as is often the case), and the visitor will normally be able to find a brochure with a few paragraphs in English on the role of the temple in Japanese history, on any unusual local beliefs with which the temple is associated, and on famous people or works of art connected with it. Buddhist temples in Japan can be grouped under four general headings according to how they are used and the functions they fulfill.

The first category is that of *ekō* temples, which serve as centers for funeral and memorial services. They are really parish temples, and their priests regard themselves as having territorial responsibility for the families which are registered with them as subscribers. These temples are most easily recognized in the countryside, where they are normally surrounded by a graveyard like rural churches in Europe. The connection between a family and a temple sometimes goes back to the Edo period (1600–1867), when under the *danka* system all families were required to register at a local temple. This system still provides temple priests with the basic information on which to calculate the number of subscribers and adherents under their pastoral care. In practice it means that the priest may feel entitled to go to any or all of these families to request financial assistance for the repair of the temple roof, for example, or the purchase of a new bell, or the rebuilding of a gate or wall. It quite often happens that wealthy patrons donate large sums of money or an expensive gift to the temple or even pay for the erection of a new building. In these ways, temples keep in touch with their parishioners and remain solvent. The vast majority of temples of the Jōdo-Shin sect fall into this category, and they derive their income principally through funeral services.

Temples that are really monastic or seminarial in nature make up the second group. These usually function as the administrative headquarters of a denomination and provide training for priests of the order. The Sōtō sect of Zen has its headquarters in Fukui Prefecture at the Eihei-ji, while the Rinzai sect has a head temple for each of its subsects: the Nanzen-ji and Kennin-ji in Kyoto and the Kenchō-ji in Kamakura prominent among them. The Zōjō-ji in Tokyo is the head temple of the largest wing of the Jōdo sect, and the Nishi (west) Hongan-ji and Higashi (east) Hongan-ji in Kyoto are the headquarters of their respective wings of the Jōdo-Shin sect. The head temple of the Nichiren sect, the Kuon-ji, stands on a peak near Mount Fuji, and the great monastery complexes on Mount Hiei and Mount Kōya are the centers of Tendai and Shingon Buddhism respectively. Not all of these temples are easy to visit. The Eihei-ji for one, however, permits guests—providing they agree to conform to the strict rules of the temple, which include lights out at nine in the evening and a three o'clock reveille.

The third category consists of temples in ancient cities like Nara, Kyoto, and Kamakura that nowadays are little more than examples of outstanding architecture or treasure houses of great works of Buddhist art. Some of them still have resident priests, who occasionally conduct ceremonies. They belong, like all temples in Japan, to a sect but may well no longer have any parishioners. Tourists provide the bulk of their income, and among tourists the sober black-and-white or navy-blue-and-white uniforms of schoolchildren are likely to be conspicuous.

The fourth group is made up of temples for prayer and devotion, known as *kitō* temples. The protective function remains an important aspect of the role of these temples, and people go to them to pray for success in business or recovery from illness in the way we examined at the be-

8. Each of these little statues of the bodhisattva Jizō (*left*) is dedicated to the memory of a different child, for Jizō is the guardian of the spirits of dead children. These statues stand in the grounds of the Zōjō-ji, one of the biggest temples in Tokyo, under the shadow of the Tokyo Tower (see back end-paper).

9. Legend has it that when the historical Buddha was born nectar rained from the sky, and this is why to this day people celebrate the Buddha's birthday by pouring sweet tea over his image (*above*), which is placed in a specially built, flower-bedecked shrine. The celebrations have been held in Japan each year since the early seventh century, when they were introduced from China.

10. Buddhism in Japan has always been closely connected with health and healing. In early centuries, Yakushi, the Buddha of medicine, was one of the most popular of Buddhist deities, and sutras were chanted to bring an end to epidemics. Nowadays worshipers still go regularly to temples in search of a cure for various ailments. Many temples have a large incense burner in the middle of the forecourt, and a common form of therapy, seen here practiced at the Tō-ji in Kyoto (*right*), involves drawing fumes from the censer over the part of the body that is causing pain.

ginning of this chapter. Temples of the esoteric sects, Shingon and Tendai, and Nichiren temples in particular specialize in these activities, although some of them may have local, parochial support as well. The priests who perform the requested ceremonies for individual worshipers have in some cases undergone special training, and some may even have mastered certain secrets of Buddhism through which they can confer powers or blessings on those who consult them. In this category too are the temples that house a special image of Jizō, Kannon, or some other popular deity to whom people come to pray.

Temple Life

Of the various Buddhist sects in Japan, the Pure Land sects—Jōdo and Jōdo-Shin and their various branches—have by far the largest number of temples, 30,312 out of a total of 72,941, and they claim the largest number of adherents. If, however, the members of some of the most closely related "new religions" are added to the number of adherents claimed by the Nichiren sect, then it becomes clear that the Pure Land and Nichiren traditions represent the two major organized forces in modern Japanese Buddhism. The Zen sect has 21,118 temples, and Shingon in particular claims a large ratio of adherents to temples. Nevertheless, statistics of adherents tend to mislead, adherence normally amounting to little more than family registration at a temple.

There is no doubt, however, but that the Pure Land sects remain the most popular form of traditional Buddhism in Japan. How are they faring at present? Together with some students I undertook a survey recently and visited some Jōdo-Shin temples to interview the priests. There emerged from the answers to our questions the recognition among priests of clear changes in temple life. The days when people attended weekly sermons and regular gatherings are long past. Indeed, since the Meiji Restoration in 1868, when Japan threw out its old feudal government and feeling against Buddhism ran high, much ground has been lost. The subsequent manipulation of state Shinto also had a damaging effect on Buddhism, and today many people are highly suspicious of organized religion of any kind, domestic or foreign. What form the innate Japanese desire for religious self-expression will take in the future is a matter of much concern among priests.

One priest we interviewed, with a temple in downtown Tokyo, has a roll of about seven-hundred "parishioners." His temple belongs to the East Hongan-ji wing, which has about nine thousand out of the total of thirty-thousand temples affiliated with the Pure Land sects. People no longer showed much interest, the priest told us. Meetings of parishioners to read sutras and to talk about Buddhism attracted only about thirty or forty people, among whom there were no young people. The priest's son was attending Otani University, a Buddhist college, to be trained to succeed his father. The priest's two daughters, aged nineteen and fifteen, showed little interest in temple affairs. The picture nationwide, the priest felt, was little different.

Such feelings must be considered in perspective. While the mainline Buddhist sects are facing certain difficulties in retaining their traditional hold over people's allegiances,

Many Japanese towns grew up around markets held at temple gates. Some markets became permanent fixtures. Others—like the one shown in these photographs at Fukagawa in downtown Tokyo—are held on certain days connected with the deity worshiped at the temple.

Running nursery schools has become a common undertaking for temples.

it must be remembered that Buddhism nowadays is concerned very much with the funeral and therefore tends to have to do more with people of a mature age who are facing some of life's more difficult times, when the meaning of Buddhism may become more relevant. The years of middle age invariably bring with them—when parents die, for example—various duties involving religious observances, and there are few Japanese who find reason to rebel against religious customs involving the family.

Temple Finances

Temple finances have become an increasing problem since Buddhism lost much of its social standing at the time of the Meiji Restoration. After the constitutional separation of state and religion introduced at the end of the war, problems have become even greater. Inflation plus declining organized support have forced at least a quarter of all the temples to engage in alternative fund-raising projects such as operating apartment houses, parking lots, and even golf courses. A considerable number of temples manage their own nursery school or old people's home, with priests devoting some of their time to administering the places and helping look after the children and old people. The picture is not so vastly different from that found in the United States, where churches with financial difficulties need to raise revenue to supplement donations from church members in order to continue operating all their programs.

Nevertheless many temples in Japan are well endowed—all are tax exempt under the 1946 Religious Corporation Act—and some have for centuries owned large tracts of real estate. In these larger temples, priests are usually able to dedicate themselves fulltime to their duties. There is even a Buddhist monthly magazine that offers advice on managing estates, raising funds, and taking advantage of tax-exemption laws, as well as on ways to win back the allegiance of ordinary people.

Education and Welfare

Buddhism in Japan has a long association with education and welfare stretching back to the ideals of Prince Shōtoku. Many of Japan's oldest temples were once centers of learning. The Hōryū-ji in Nara was originally called the Hōryū-gakumon-ji (the Hōryū "temple of learning"), implying that it was as much as seminary as a monastery. The scholastic spirit of Buddhism in the eighth-century Nara period helped to strengthen the connection with education. The association continued through the centuries, and a thousand years later during the Edo period Buddhist priests offered elementary education to children in schools known as *terakoya*, where they taught reading, writing, and calculation on the abacus.

Although nowadays the state takes basic responsibility for education, there are many private institutions within the Japanese educational system, and a few of these are run by Buddhist organizations. In Kyoto, the Otani and Ryūkoku universities are run by the Jōdo-Shin sect, and in Tokyo there is Taishō University, which is affiliated with the Tendai, Shingon, and Jōdo sects, and Komazawa University, which is run by the Sōtō Zen sect. Beneath these universities is a network of junior colleges (two-year institutions), high schools, junior high schools, and elementary schools, as well as the nursery schools.

The Tsukiji Hongan-ji, Japan's only stone temple in the Indian style, located near the site of the famous fish market, does a great deal of work in the field of welfare and education. The temple organizes more than six-hundred lectures and sermons every year. People from many walks of life attend, among them company employees and businessmen, including staff from the Japanese National Railways as well as other large corporations. In keeping with the times, the temple also sponsors *kokoro no denwa,* a Buddhist version of dial-a-prayer, with callers being treated to a three-minute meditation on a sutra.

11. A priest delivers a sermon at Narita-san, a large and imposing temple near Tokyo's international airport. In medieval times, evangelists traveled the length and the breadth of the country, preaching at street corners or dancing and singing their message as they went. Preaching was once common in temples too, and, especially in the countryside, priests are often still asked to act as unofficial counselors to help solve local problems.

12. Also at Narita-san, a group of worshipers learn the art of copying sutras. In the Heian period, the copying of sutras was widely considered by members of the aristocracy to be a highly effective means of acquiring religious merit. Mention is made in *The Tale of Genji*, for instance, of copying the *Lotus Sutra*. In later centuries, the custom spread along with literacy, and the belief grew that the writing of the letters was of itself an expression of faith.

13, 14. These roly-poly, papier-mâché figures (*left*), with their white faces and red bodies, are good luck charms known as *daruma*. Their name derives from Bodhidharma, the legendary Indian patriarch who introduced Zen to China and who sat facing a wall for nine years, as a result of which he lost the use of his legs. Not a few temples—for example, here, the Jindai-ji in the west of Tokyo—have *daruma* markets, especially at the New Year. A student about to sit an exam might buy a *daruma*, and so too, almost invariably, a politician contesting an election. When he buys the *daruma*, the candidate will color in one of the eyes. If he wins the election, he colors in the other one, an event that becomes the crowning moment of the campaign. *Daruma* are normally taken back to the temple to be burnt in a giant bonfire (*below*). The *daruma* has lent its name to several similarly rotund objects: Japanese children call their snowmen *yuki* (snow) *daruma*, while their fathers refer to the distinctive black bottles of whisky as *daruma*.

15. The Sensō-ji (*right*)—with its huge lanterns, made famous to Westerners through the prints of Hiroshige—is one of the oldest and most popular temples in Tokyo. In the Edo period, the Sensō-ji and the surrounding district of Asakusa were at the very heart of the city, standing for all that was most representative of popular Edo culture. The present buildings were reconstructed in the late fifties following the original seventeenth-century design. The Sensō-ji still attracts hordes of worshipers and sightseers every day.

4 The Buddhist Funeral

In case I attain the ultimate goal of buddhahood, I vow to receive all human beings who think of me one to ten times or more sincerely wishing to be received into my Pure Land. Until I have fulfilled this vow, I will not become a Buddha but will remain a Buddha-to-be.

Amida's Original Vow

Religion of the Funeral

Mr. Tanaka, I was shocked to hear of your tragic untimely death in an automobile accident last week. All of us in the research and development section were overcome with grief. You were always very kind to us, and, when you rose in rank and position and your responsibilities became greater, you made time to talk with us and encourage us. Even when you became senior manager, you still offered us much helpful advice. Indeed, what success we are having today is due entirely to your ideas. Our success is really your success, and we will faithfully continue your policy in the future as the true expression of our respect and gratitude.

We hope you are at peace. We thank you for your help and pray that we continue to benefit from your inspiration. We pray for the happy repose of your soul.

These words I offer sincerely on behalf of the members of the research and development section of Heiwa Research Company.

If you attend a funeral ceremony in Japan, the chances are you will hear a speech similar to this addressed to the deceased, paying tribute, showing respect, and saying that the Buddha has been invoked so that the soul of the departed may be eternally at peace.

As this speech suggests, the relationship between the living and the dead in Japan is quite different from the sort of relationship with which Americans and Europeans are familiar. At the root of this difference lie two fascinating aspects of Buddhism in Japan: its long and intimate relationship with death on the one hand, and, on the other, its sensitive way of expressing the continuity of the relationship between the living and the dead.

Buddhism here can be seen fulfilling one of the essential roles of religion, that of acting as a binding force in society (the word "religion" itself is derived from a Latin verb meaning "to bind"). In the West religion has be-

come increasingly a personal concern and so has lost much of its force as a binding power. In Japan, however, it has retained its relevance to the family and society as a whole. Buddhism's social function is most apparent in its association with the funeral and death.

Of all the aspects of human existence, there is none in which we have a greater need for a binding force than death. We need a socially sanctioned "death system," in which all the words, rituals, and symbols of death relate to each other to form a structure that gives meaning to death as well as comfort and support to the bereaved. This need is well documented in a book called *The American Way of Death* (see Bibliography), in which the author, Jessica Mitford, shows us what happens when religion loses its social role and commercial interests take its place. That this has not occurred in Japan can be attributed to the long connection between Buddhism and death, a connection which results both from certain tendencies within Buddhism itself and from its success in filling this role in Japanese society.

Amida and the Pure Land

Buddhist priests have been conducting funeral services on a regular basis (at least in part in order to augment their incomes) since the thirteenth century. The connection, however, dates back well before then, and its origins can be traced to the earliest days of Buddhism in Japan. Indeed, the Buddha Amida and the bodhisattva Jizō were associated with death even before belief in them had been transmitted to Japan. A sutra connected with Amida, the *Amida Sutra*, was recited at the imperial court as early as the year 640, and the emperor Uda (866–931) is reported to have died invoking the name of Amida. Already at this time, a funeral according to Buddhist rites was popular among members of the aristocracy.

It was as a result of popular feeling, however, that the worship of Amida flourished to the level where it became a nationwide cult. The ground for this development was laid early: in the seventh and eighth centuries, there were many monks traveling around the country preaching life after death through faith in Amida. But the decisive development came in the Kamakura period, when Hōnen (1133–1212) and his followers, in the face of opposition from the established clergy in Nara and Kyoto and of repression and persecution from the government, made it clear through their own success that the people's faith in Amida had become a deeply entrenched expression of popular religious feeling (pl. 20).

For Hōnen the essence of religious practice lay in the recitation of the name of Amida Buddha. Out of this grew the Pure Land tradition first of the Jōdo sect, which was formed by the followers of Hōnen, and later of the Jodō-Shin sect, which grew out of the further simplification of Buddhist thought effected by Hōnen's disciple Shinran (1173–1262). Shinran was a priest of the Tendai school whose association with Hōnen inspired him to further radicalize and simplify Hōnen's doctrine. According to Shinran it was not even necessary to recite the name of Amida, for Amida had made a vow, the Original Vow (*hongan*), to save all mankind; it was Amida's decision to save us and not our faith in Amida that mattered. Appropriately, Shinran is buried in the Hongan-ji, the "temple of the Original Vow," in Kyoto.

Another of Shinran's innovations was to do away with celibacy for priests (he himself was married) in order to stress the equality of all people in relation to Amida's Original Vow. A result of this reform was to enable the development of the tradition of family ownership of temples on a hereditary basis, as with Shinto shrines. Initially, however, priests of the Pure Land sects possessed neither land nor wealth, let alone temples, and as a result they became closely connected with funeral and postfuneral rites, which they performed for the families of the common people.

Although Amida and the funeral are closely connected with the Pure Land sects, they are by no means confined to this tradition. On the contrary, such was the impact of the Amida cult that by the fourteenth century, even the highly sophisticated Zen school became more attentive to popular needs and devoted a large number of treatises to the subject of how to conduct funeral services properly.

Guiding the Dead to Paradise

The concept of rebirth for all in Amida's Pure Land paradise has come to have a strong and lasting influence on Japanese attitudes toward death and the funeral itself, for rebirth in paradise means rebirth as a Buddha, and appropriate preparations must therefore be made. The function of the priest is to guide the dead to paradise through a series of rituals that vary from one sect to another according to basic doctrinal differences but that nevertheless have a lot in common.

The *kaimyō*, or posthumous name, is an important element in the rites connected with death. As a term, *kaimyō*

Shinran, from a near-contemporary scroll.

refers not only, however, to the name conferred on people who have just died but also to the name traditionally given to young monks on ordination. In a corresponding way, the deceased is in certain cases actually initiated into the priesthood, an event that is sometimes accompanied by a symbolic shaving of the head. In a general context, dead persons are often referred to as *hotoke*, the native Japanese word for a Buddha. Even a police officer marking a chalk line around the victim of a traffic accident will refer to the dead person as *hotoke-san*, "honorable Buddha."

The Buddhist funeral thus becomes an occasion on which the dead person is assured not only of entry into paradise but also of immediate buddhahood as well. Unlike reincarnation, which never really caught on in Japan except as a means of exhorting people to lead a better life, the concept of entry into paradise and immediate buddhahood is fully in accord with traditional Japanese feelings of reverence for ancestors, especially as it does not interfere with the possibility of becoming an ancestral *kami*.

The Journey to the Grave

What usually takes place when someone dies in Japan? It is still the custom in most families to consult a priest. This done, arrangements are made for the first of a series of

16

17

18

19

Distance and the small size of city houses and apartments has meant that arrangements for funerals have become more flexible in recent decades. It is often no longer possible for everyone invited to attend a funeral the day after someone's death. This is especially the case when the deceased held a position of professional or social prominence, in which case the number of friends and acquaintances would most likely make different arrangements necessary. As a result, what tends to happen is that the funeral itself is an intimate affair for family members, relatives, and close friends. Then a week or two later, a larger memorial ceremony is held in a temple or a special funeral hall like the Aoyama *saijō* in central Tokyo, where these photographs were taken. Although the scale is different from a funeral ceremony at home, the memorial service proceeds in a similar fashion (pl. 16). The first part of the service —the reading from a sutra and offering of prayers to the deceased— is conducted by the priest. This is followed by funeral addresses like the one on page 36 delivered by mourners to the deceased (pl. 17) and the lighting of incense (pls. 18, 19). From a practical point of view, one of the most important and helpful customs associated with the funeral is that in which mourners offer a gift of money to the bereaved. This often turns out to be a welcome source of income, especially if the bereaved is an elderly person.

The eleventh-century Phoenix Hall in Uji, south of Kyoto, is modeled after pictorial representations of Amida's palace in the Western Paradise. The heavenly serenity of the architecture is complemented inside the hall by a gilded statue of Amida surrounded by angels descending to earth to welcome the soul of a dying believer.

ceremonies, called *otsuya*, the equivalent of a wake. An altar is rented and set up in front of where the deceased is lying in his or her coffin. In the middle of the altar is placed a photograph of the deceased, a photograph that will have been specially taken for this purpose—everyone has a photograph taken to be placed on the funeral altar when he or she dies.

Family and close friends gather, and the priest arrives and offers prayers to the departed. The mourners then offer a pinch of incense, this being the symbolic way of saluting a Buddha. Incense, in fact, plays an important part in all matters concerning the dead, whether during the funeral, at the grave, or by the ancestral altar. Friends may also take the chance now to talk a little with the deceased, since there is scarcely time for close personal greetings during the public funeral.

If arrangements can be made in time, the formal public service is held on the following day (pls. 16–19). The assembled mourners stand outside the house (the outer screens and door are removed or opened so that all can see what is going on), while the priest, inside at the altar surrounded by close family members, reads from an appropriate sutra and offers prayers to the departed. When the priest is finished, the chief mourner recites the personal history of the deceased. Then comes the moment when friends and colleagues address the dead person in memorial speeches such as the one at the beginning of this chapter, in which they express sentiments of sadness and gratitude and extend their wishes for his or her well-being. When the speeches are all over, the mourners approach the altar one by one, make a bow of respect, and offer incense once more. Now the main ceremony, which takes place at the dead person's

house, is over and the mourners all head for the temple and cemetery by car or on foot, depending on whether they live in a town or in the country.

In the country it is still normal practice to form a procession according to the traditions of the community or sect and walk in order to the temple. Flowers, paper dragons on poles, and sometimes musicians with cymbals and gongs precede the priests, who are followed by the principal mourners carrying the photograph of the deceased, the incense burner, a *tōba* (wooden post notched near the top with the names of the five elements of existence written in Sanskrit), the coffin, and various offerings of food. Before entering the temple building, the procession winds its way three times round the temple forecourt, a symbol of passing the gates into nirvana. Incense is again offered, and the mourners then depart, leaving only close family members in attendance.

If a family has lived for a long time in the area, the body of the deceased may well be interred in the temple graveyard. It may also, however, be taken for cremation, a custom introduced into Japan through Buddhism and now widely adopted because of lack of space. The bones of the dead are especially precious, and after cremation they are ceremonially removed from the ashes with chopsticks by a relative, who then uses another set of chopsticks to place them in an urn. (This is why Japanese shudder if they see anything passed directly from one set of chopsticks to another.) The *tōba* is then set up at the grave, water poured over it, food laid out, and incense sticks set alight.

Unlike in the West, where mourning nowadays often ends at the grave, the funeral is only the first in a series of observances which I shall discuss in the following chapter.

5 The Welfare of the Dead

*Even the virtuous can attain rebirth in the Pure Land,
so how much more so the wicked.*

Shinran

Butsudan—The Altar for Ancestors

Nihon no kokoro, "the heart of Japan," read the characters inscribed prominently on a poster by the roadside. What were they advertising? A trip to Kyoto, to Nikko, or to the Ise shrines? Or maybe lessons in the tea ceremony or flower arrangement? No, none of these things; the "heart of Japan" was a *butsudan*, the Buddhist family altar that can be found in homes in all parts of the country. The *butsudan* is the place where the ancestors of the household are enshrined, fed, tended, and revered by the living (pl. 27).

Butsudan are a common feature in Japanese houses, and in the rare cases where space permits they form the centerpiece of a whole room, known as a *butsuma*. Often however the same room contains, as well as the *butsudan*, a *kamidana* ("shelf" for the Shinto *kami*), which exists to protect the home, the community, or the locality. The *kami* enshrined there may include some ancestors but not necessarily immediate family forebears. Offerings to the *kami* normally include rice cakes, fish, *sake*, and vegetables, but those at the *butsudan* are in keeping with the Buddhist proscription on the taking of life and therefore are usually limited to cooked rice, water (no alcoholic drinks), and perhaps a small sweet or candy.

The relations with the *kami* tend to be different, less personal and more concerned with the locality than those with the direct family ancestors to whom respect is paid at the *butsudan*. But this difference aside, it is here, in the cult of the ancestor, that Buddhism and Shinto show a unity of approach. The importance of paying reverence to one's forebears predates the arrival of Buddhism in Japan, but, since Buddhism had already accommodated itself to a similar attitude in China, it had less trouble adjusting itself to the ancestor cult in Japan. Japanese folk religion included the belief that the dead live in a world parallel to that of the living. It was also believed that the happiness of the living depended on the happiness of the dead and that this depended on the degree and success with which the living propitiated the dead by serving them, asking their advice, and obeying their wishes.

The first recorded reference to Buddhist altars in the home is found in an imperial edict issued in 685 and quoted in the eighth-century *Chronicles of Japan* decreeing that "in every house a Buddhist altar should be established, and an image of Buddha with Buddhist scriptures placed there. Worship is to be paid and food offered at these altars." The *butsudan* is still the focal point for Buddhist ceremonies in the home and particularly of postfuneral ceremonies and rituals. It is most likely to be found in the house of the oldest surviving male member of the family; with possession of the *butsudan* goes the responsibility for maintaining the family grave.

Attitudes toward Ancestors in Modern Japan

Do the Japanese still revere their ancestors and offer food and incense on the family altar? The answer is yes. One American scholar who has done research in this field reports that he was treated to some cynical comments from his colleagues before leaving to investigate contemporary attitudes in Japan. "Don't waste your time. You won't find any ancestral altars in Tokyo," they told him (this was in 1962). But he did. Ten years later, when he announced that he was going back to Japan for further research, the reaction was similar: "Well, you may have found ancestral altars in Tokyo ten years ago," they said, "but you can be sure there aren't any left now." They were wrong again. About half the households he investigated in Tokyo still possessed an altar or, at the least, some objects used in paying respect to ancestors. When one considers that a large percentage of the population of Tokyo is resident there for purposes of employment only, having a hometown elsewhere, half is indeed a lot. Moreover, research by other scholars in rural Japan suggests that the percentage in the countryside is nearer eighty percent. To come further up to date, the president of the company whose advertisement for *butsudan* caught my eye published in 1981 the first major comprehensive work giving a detailed account of *butsudan* and how to use and look after them according to the many and various customs of the different sects.

The crucial concept that underlies both the Japanese

20. The great statue of Amida at Kamakura (*left*) stands over eleven meters high, slightly smaller but, most people would agree, more beautiful than the Nara *daibutsu* at the Tōdai-ji (pl. 3). It was once enclosed within the main hall of the Kōtoku-in, the temple in whose grounds it still stands, but the building was swept away by a tidal wave in 1495. The statue is cast in bronze—a considerable technological feat for the thirteenth century—and was completed in 1252. Unlike the Nara *daibutsu*, which was the product of a financial and artistic effort orchestrated by the state, funds for the construction of this, the Kamakura *daibutsu*, were donated by the faithful, and the whole thing was planned by a priest named Jōkō. It soon became the supreme symbol of the cult of Amida and the forerunner of other large statues of Buddhas erected in various parts of the country.

21. In contrast to the bliss of Amida's Western Paradise is the torment of hell, which is presided over by Emma, the king of hell (*above*). Emma's origins are obscure but can be traced back to Indian myth and folk religion. He took a peripheral position in the Buddhist pantheon with the decline in the belief in reincarnation. Emma has remained an object of terror and hence a shadowy figure who has never won affection or popularity. He is often depicted in works of art meting out "justice" to the souls of the departed. Here he is flanked by two assistants and the Ten Kings (of whom he is one), figures from Chinese folk religion. The statues belong to the Tōkō-ji, a temple in Kisarazu, Chiba Prefecture.

22. One of the holiest mountains in Japan is Osore-zan (*right*) in the far north of the country. As its name suggests (Osore-zan means "mountain of fear"), the area is awesomely wild and desolate. These piles of stone were built, so the belief goes, by the spirits of dead children on the bed of the river they must cross to reach the land of the departed. The lucky ones among the children will be saved by the bodhisattva Jizō, but those who linger too long on the riverbed will be snatched up by demons and dragged off to hell.

The job of selling Buddhist furniture has become big business. Prices for the *butsudan* in this full-page advertisement range from a mere $250 to as much as $5,000. In downtown Tokyo, the best part of the stores lining one of the main streets deal in *butsudan*.

attitude of reverence toward ancestors and the *butsudan*, symbol of this reverence, is that the dead continue to exist in some form and that the happiness and well-being of the living depend on the happiness and well-being of the dead. Lafcadio Hearn, who settled in a remote part of the west of Japan in the latter years of the nineteenth century and wrote with love and insight on his adopted country, tells a story that nicely illustrates Japanese attitudes toward the dead. While correcting some English sentences written by his students, he came across the words "being faithful to our ancestors," instead of which he recommended "being faithful to *the memory of* our ancestors." This, Hearn was told, was not what the students really wanted to say, and he realized they were speaking in a way that treated the ancestors as though they were living and present.

Postfuneral Rites

Japanese concern for the well-being of ancestors is shown at the family grave as well as at the household altar. Of the duties involving the grave, some are postfuneral rites, whereas others are regular annual events. The postfuneral

rites are centered on seventh-day observances, of which there are seven in all. Each of these seventh-day observances used to involve a visit to the grave, but nowadays only the first is adhered to with full formality, while the last, known as the *shi-jū-ku nichi* because it comes on the "forty-ninth day" after the death, is also considered to be of great importance. In some parts of Japan, the belief still exists that the dead person's soul remains in the house until the forty-ninth day, after which it leaves for paradise. During these forty-nine days, which constitute the principal period of mourning, certain observances are adhered to, some of which, such as a vegetarian diet, reflect Buddhist customs, while others derive from the Shinto belief that death is a form of impurity—for example, invitations to weddings are rejected and no celebrations are made at the New Year.

Details vary from one part of Japan to another, but, generally after the forty-ninth day, the memorial tablet bearing the posthumous name of the deceased is placed in the *butsudan*. The wooden post at the grave is replaced by a gravestone normally after at least a year has elapsed, and thereafter the grave-side ceremonies become more of a formality.

Once the period of mourning is over, three types of ceremony are usually performed. These are the monthly commemorations, called *mai tsuki mei nichi*, the annual commemoration, *shō tsuki mei nichi*, and the periodic ceremonies, or *nenki*, which are held on various anniversaries, including the first, third, seventh, thirteenth, twenty-third, twenty-seventh, and so on, culminating in the hundredth anniversary ceremony. By this time, however, most of the original mourners themselves are dead, and so in modern times these ceremonies tend to merge into the communal forms of annual reverence paid to ancestors: grave visiting (*ohakamairi*) on the equinox (pls. 23–25) and the festival of *obon*, the Japanese All Souls' Day.

Ohakamairi, "Grave Visiting"

It is a custom throughout Japan for families to visit the grave at least twice a year, during *higan*, the name for the weeks in which the spring and autumn equinoxes occur. Families take offerings of food and flowers, as well as a container for water, which they fill up at the cemetery, pouring the water over the gravestone to cleanse it. In addition to the food and the flowers, which are placed at the gravestone, sticks of incense are lit and placed in cups or jars by the grave. And if the cemetery is in the country or in a small town, members of a family may do the rounds, offering food, flowers, and incense at the graves of relatives and perhaps finally at the memorial tablet to the war dead.

Grave visiting is still a leisurely event, and families who have traveled some distance to reach the cemetery may well decide to have a picnic while they are there. The Western mind can conceive without difficulty of taking flowers to the grave but not food. If communion with the dead is possible, however, then there is no contradiction involved in feeding the dead and eating there oneself. Therein lies a basic difference in the perception of death. The grave is a place of importance for the Japanese of today in just the same way that the mountains were in days of old, when it was believed that the spirits of the dead resided there. The dead interact with the living; this is the principle that energizes the system.

Caring for the Dead

Images come to mind of Japanese friends and relatives of mine who have shown a concern and affection for departed members of their families and have maintained a quietly profound relationship that typifies the attitude of the Japanese toward their dead. I remember a young woman I once knew, bereaved of her mother, leaving a party early in order to have dinner with her mother as she always had done. When she cooked rice for herself, she would offer some to the *butsudan* before she ate her own portion. Another friend, a widower, confided to me that in the evening he would sit down beside the *butsudan* to read his book because he felt less lonely there.

Buddhism thus offers a constructive system of support for the bereaved that is—in terms of thanatology—both psychologically sound because it focuses the attention of the living on participatory activity and effective in giving the feeling of being close to the dead. Christianity espouses the idea of resurrection from the dead, the defiance of death by the grace and power of God—death, in the Christian tradition, being the result of sin, a punishment from God. In contrast, there exists in Japan a belief in the continuing presence of the dead, a metaphysic "denying" rather than "defying" the finality of death. The discord of death is reset into a key that makes melodious what is a source of disharmony in the West. Death represents the last stage in a process that sees the spirit of the dead become a *hotoke*, or Buddha, whose presence is invisible but whose influence continues to be felt.

When the late Prime Minister Ohira died during the election campaign of 1980, some political analysts thought his Liberal Democratic Party might suffer a reverse as a result of the loss of its leader. But they had forgotten the power of the tradition of reverence for the dead. Despite running on policies that included tax increases—policies that might well have lost votes had Ohira lived—the party won with an increased majority, and Ohira's successor, Suzuki Zenkō pledged to carry out his predecessor's plans. On the day of the victory, party leaders gathered round an enlarged death portrait of their former leader and, to the customary shouts of *banzai*, posed for the cameras (pl. 26).

One branch of the Amida cult was founded by Ippen (1239–89), who encouraged his followers to dance while chanting "*Namu Amida butsu*" (Hail to the Buddha Amida). This scene in the streets of Kyoto is part of a scroll depicting Ippen's life.

23–25. At a large cemetery in the north of Tokyo, the old and the young, parents and children visit the family grave during the autumn *higan*, the week in which the equinox occurs. *Higan*, which means the "other shore," in other words paradise, was first celebrated as a result of an imperial decree issued in the year 806. It was not until a few cen- turies ago, however, that observances for *higan* began to include a visit to the family grave. The choice of the equinox as a time to celebrate *higan* is thought to be connected with the idea of change and imper- manence suggested by these "landmarks" of the passing seasons.

充実への挑戦

26. Colleagues of the late Prime Minister Ohira celebrate the Liberal Democratic Party's victory in the 1980 general election with the death portrait of their former party leader. Standing above the portrait on the left is Ohira's successor as prime minister, Suzuki Zenkō, and on the right, Sakurauchi Yoshio, who was party secretary-general at the time.

27. Lighting the incense is one of the rites performed every day at a *butsudan*, the Buddhist altar for ancestors (*right*). First, however, candles are lit, a bell is rung, and hands are clapped to draw the attention of the ancestors' spirits. After the incense has been lit and placed in its stand, the name of Amida or of the *Lotus Sutra*—depending on the sect to which the worshiper's family belongs—is recited, and finally a few private prayers are said. The *butsudan* in the photograph has a tray in front of it set out with fruit and vegetables for the festival of *obon*. Inside the *butsudan* are wooden tablets with the posthumous names of family ancestors, dishes for water and rice, a small incense burner, a candle holder, a flower of metal, and an image of a Buddhist deity.

6 Buddhism and the Japanese Character

All that exists is impermanent;

All elements are selfless;

Nirvana is serenity, peace.

The Great Wisdom Sutra

Patience amidst Change

The stock image people have of the Japanese character is often connected with the idea of discipline, something to do maybe with the martial spirit. Customs that gave rise to this image of the Japanese are not hard to find: company employees taking part in exercises at 8:30 in the morning, for example, or attending evening classes in karate or judo or *kendō* (Japanese fencing). Some of this indeed is a result of the influence of Buddhism, the kind of Buddhism that first attracted the interest of the warrior classes in the thirteenth century. The Japanese, however, have many other attributes that we tend to think of as "typical" and that can be ascribed at least in part to Buddhist concepts. Among these, for example, the never-failing Japanese smile, the aptitude for patiently enduring unpleasant experiences, and the ability to remain contented in a world of change and uncertainty can all be traced to Buddhism—to a Buddhist resignation that encourages people to accept the world with its suffering as it is.

Buddhist concepts have permeated the social psychology of the Japanese in various ways, giving it many of the features that experts in fields such as communication studies and body language find distinctively Japanese. The impressions gained by common observation are often supported by the testimony of experts. Behavioral scientists, for instance, agree that the Japanese remain patient and disciplined to a much greater degree than is to be found in most Western societies. Crowd control at large spectator sports events or in crowded railway stations is much less a matter of anxiety than it is in Europe or America. Although in the external manifestations of modern culture, the Japanese appear to have become pretty thoroughly Westernized, attitudes and values remain distinctively Japanese as a result of the country's cultural and social homogeneity. Japanese society, it seems, has learnt to combine the dynamics of change with a kind of conservatism, a combination that makes for stability and continuity. One element that has helped to create this successful combination has been the formless but pervasive presence of a Buddhist outlook and Buddhist ideals.

Buddhism in Everyday Expressions

Expressions used in everyday circumstances provide an excellent example of the omnipresence of Buddhist values in Japanese life. In a similar sort of way, the English language is full of expressions with Biblical origins, like "salt of the earth" and "the good Samaritan," expressions which we often use without considering their derivation. A classic case of a Japanese proverb that contains a cherished Buddhist concept is:

> *Sode furi-au mo tashō no en.*
> "Even brushing sleeves with someone as you pass by is the result of a connection in a previous existence."

En in the vocabulary of Japanese Buddhism refers to the causes that bring about the results we can see and experience in the present. A *kahō no yoi hito* is someone whose *kahō* (the results, usually of a favorable kind, produced by *en*) is good (*yoi*)—in other words, a lucky person. A warning about perfection comes in the words *Kōbō Daishi ni mo fude no ayamari*—even Kōbō Daishi (the name by which Kūkai, founder of the Shingon sect, is commonly known) could make a slip of the pen. The bodhisattva Jizō appears in many proverbs and expressions:

> *Karu toki no Jizō-gao; nasu toki no Emma-gao.*
> "When we borrow something, we look contented, like Jizō; when we pay back, our faces are like Emma, the king of hell."

Some of the simplest and commonest expressions of everyday language also carry a Buddhist nuance. A polite greeting of the sort used in everyday speech might go as follows:

Ogenki desu ka?	"How are you?"
Okagesama de genki desu.	"Praise be, I'm fine."

Okagesama implies the beneficent cooperation of powers and agencies beyond those possessed by the individual himself and the idea of dependence on a kind of divine grace. The same might be said of the expression Japanese use before eating, *itadakimasu*, which literally means "I will receive" but which also carries an implication of dependence on the part of the receiver upon the mercy of the giver, human or otherwise. The beneficence of Buddha is thus appealed to in these simple expressions of respect.

Japanese proverbs have also come to express Buddhist and Confucian social values; for example, the way in which relationships are structured according to the vertical priorities of obligation rather than the spiritual ideals that are so highly valued in the West. An old Buddhist proverb puts it this way:

> *Oyako wa isse, fūfū wa nise, shujū wa sanze.*
> "The relationship between parent and child holds for life, that between husband and wife for this life and after death, but the relationship between lord and retainer holds good before birth, during life, and after death."

Something of the sentiment expressed in this proverb survives in the loyalty shown by many Japanese salaried workers to their company.

Bills left by pilgrims to the Sensō-ji in Tokyo.

The Three Marks of Existence

Buddhism has an external, concrete presence in its temples, its statues, and its roadside altars; it has imparted its own flavor to the Japanese language; and it has taken root in Japanese attitudes toward the individual and society. Buddha identified three distinguishing marks of human existence that were intended to help people understand the Eightfold Path he taught. The first of the three marks corresponds to the first Noble Truth: that the universe and, therefore, all of human life is permeated by suffering. What this has come to mean for the Japanese is that life will always be imperfect in terms of personal happiness and satisfaction and that it is often necessary to put up with less than might have been hoped for.

The acceptance in Japan of this principle, which would be intolerable for anyone who believes in the right to hap-

Preparations for opening time in big stores reveal something of the Buddhist-influenced preference for merging into a group identity.

piness, was made possible by the successful implantation into Japanese social psychology of the other two marks: the belief that the existence of the self is an illusion and, secondly, that since everything is in a state of change nothing is permanent anyway. These concepts are reflected in the attitudes of Japanese and the structure of Japanese society. And—perhaps without always having been recognized for what they are—they have attracted the attention of sociologists such as Ezra Vogel, economists such as Kenneth Boulding, and futurologists, including Hermann Kahn and Alvin Toffler.

Muga—Denial of Self

The Sanskrit term *anatman* is rendered in Japanese as *muga*—literally, "no self." *Muga* represents the belief that the individual self does not exist and that our concept of self is based on illusion. Buddhism regards individualism, especially the type fostered in the West, as a disease, because it puts limits on love and mercy in society. Japanese society eschews individualism—at least, the kind that disrupts harmony and encourages self-assertiveness. The rejection of individualism as a basic norm for the social order is one contributing factor toward the Japanese preference, whether working at home or traveling abroad, for the group. Critics of Japanese "groupism" tend to focus on the plight of the nonconformist, the outsider. I too have done so in my studies on suicide in Japan, studies that have led me to conclude that a little more flexibility at all levels of society would make life more tolerable for a large number of people who feel genuinely stifled. But such observations, however well founded they may be, show only the negative side of the picture. It can be stated with equal emphasis that, in keeping with the spirit of Buddhism, Japanese group consciousness is not merely a collectivism

28. There is a widespread popular belief that you will not be reborn in paradise if you do not at least once in your life visit the Zenkō-ji (*left*), the temple that dominates the city of Nagano in the Japanese Alps. Groups of worshipers come here from all over the country, and nearly everyone files around an unlit corridor under the main temple building (shown in the photograph) to touch a sacred key, thereby ensuring themselves a place in paradise. A well-known proverb connected with the temple derives from the story of an old woman who gave chase to an ox that made off with a cloth she had hung out to bleach. Finding herself unwittingly in the grounds of the Zenkō-ji, she forgot all about the ox and became immersed in prayer for her own salvation. The proverb—*ushi ni hikarete Zenkō-ji mairi,* "to pray at the Zenkō-ji, led there by an ox"—refers to a chance occurrence having an adventitious but beneficial outcome.

29. Followers of the Jōdo-Shin sect who wish to obtain the status of priest have their heads shaved in a ceremony known as *kikkyō-shiki.* Nowadays, the shaving of the head is often only performed symbolically; but, as can be seen in this photograph (taken at the East Hongan-ji, head temple of one wing of the Jōdo-Shin sect), some go through the full traditional ritual. In all likelihood, none of the men, women, and children in this photograph have had any formal training, for the priesthood is indeed a priesthood of all believers.

Discussing repairs at the Heirin-ji, a Rinzai Zen temple on the northwestern outskirts of Tokyo.

imposed by society upon individual people but rather the result of the rejection of "selfhood" in favor of "grouphood" as the framework for human identity.

A preference for living in a group-oriented society has given the Japanese a special talent for teamwork, a talent that has, for example, played no small part in the success of Japanese research and development programs. In this way, it might be argued that Buddhism and Japan's postwar economic miracle are not so far apart as is sometimes thought. Traditional cultural patterns often survive the upheavals of political and economic modernization, and in Japan their survival has had a positive effect on the country's drive to reestablish itself as a prominent force in world affairs.

There is another way in which this preference for the group is linked to Buddhism, involving one of the Three Buddhist Treasures, the Community of monks. The Japanese word for a monk, *biku*, which derives directly from the Sanskrit, means "one who shares." It describes the role of the Buddhist follower whose sacramental begging as an act of devotion entitles him to a share in community life and wealth in return for what he renounces. He has not contracted out of society but has accepted limitations upon himself in the form of a renunciation of certain expectations, in return for which he receives compensation. Like the Buddhist monk, the Japanese company employee belongs to a community in which, in return for renouncing certain things, he receives support in the form of job security, housing loans, and educational and welfare services for himself and his family.

Ezra Vogel has pointed out that underneath the Japanese ideal of group solidarity lies the belief that everyone gains from restraining egoism. Buddhism in this sense has had a profound influence on the Japanese way of life and, as a model for social psychology, is worth more attention than it has so far received.

Mujō—The Impermanence of Life

Mujō, a translation of the Sanskrit word *anicca*, expresses the concept that the world is a process, endlessly changing and disappearing. Things arise and fade without ever having a distinct existence of their own. We may in our imagination "freeze" a flower in blossom, but in fact the flower is merely midway between growth and decay. Again, no one ever steps into the same river twice: its flow, like the flow of life, ensures endless change. If we attach a lamp to the end of a rope and swing it in a circle, where is the real lamp and where is the path of its light? Distinctions are at best artificial things. The realization of this and its absorption into their outlook on life has given the Japanese a profound sense of *mujō*, the "impermanence" of life, of a feeling that not only flowers but also beauty, wealth, and success must all fade and disappear.

The Japanese have expressed in many works of art and literature this feeling for the impermanence of life. The fall from power of mighty families has inspired great romances like *The Tale of the Heike*, while the blossoms of spring and the colors of autumn have formed the subject of countless paintings, each of them in their way an expression of the Buddhist sense of life's transience.

7 Philosophy, Literature, and Art

Our attainment of enlightenment is something like the reflection of the moon in water. . . .
Though the light of the moon is vast and immense, it finds a home in water only a foot
long and an inch wide. The whole moon and the whole sky find room enough in a single
dewdrop, a single drop of water.

Dōgen, founder of the Sōtō Zen sect

A Philosophy in Search of a Religion

The extent to which Buddhist ideas such as the nonexistence of self and the impermanence of all living things have entered the fabric of Japanese life strongly suggests that Buddhism is something more than a religion of ceremonial and protection. It can indeed be seen not as a religion at all but rather as a psychosocial philosophy designed to assist people to understand themselves and their relation to the world and to view both in such a way as to minimize suffering and anxiety. Buddha, after all, was not a god, and his enlightenment was not an act of supernatural revelation. The idea of worshiping Buddhas and praying to them was the result of the meeting between Mahayana Buddhism and the indigenous religions of Asia. It was, in other words, in the course of being the builder of oriental civilization that Buddhism gradually grew into an institutionalized religion.

The philosopher and mathematician Alfred North Whitehead pointed to a fundamental difference between Christianity and Buddhism when he said that Christianity was a religion in search of a metaphysic with which to interpret itself whereas Buddhism was the reverse, a metaphysical system seeking to become a religion in order to express itself. While this is perhaps something of an oversimplification, these broad lines of contrast help in trying to understand why such distinct types of Buddhism exist in Japan. They help to explain why the sort of Buddhism which is an outlet for the spirituality of the ordinary people can coexist with the Buddhism that is the expression of a high degree of intellectual and aesthetic sophistication.

There continues to exist in Japan a tradition of Buddhist philosophy that is highly sophisticated and intellectually versatile. This philosophical Buddhism is a property of all the schools and sects, something that arises out of the ancient sutras and the arguments they propound. It even contains many points where parallels can be drawn with post-Cartesian Western philosophy. These similarities are best thought of as existing, not because of any historical influences of one tradition upon the other but rather as examples of the way in which the community of truth draws people from all civilizations and ages as they reflect deeply and ponder the mysterious universe around them.

The idea that personal identity is an illusion did not make its appearance in Western philosophy until the time of the eighteenth-century Scottish philosopher David Hume and his *Treatise of Human Nature*. In the twentieth century, the great movement in the United States called "process thought," which began in 1929 with the publication of Whitehead's *Process and Reality: An Essay in Cosmology*, expounded ideas that bear a strong resemblance to the cardinal Buddhist concept of the organic interrelatedness of all phenomena in the universe.

Western man, who in recent centuries has come to believe in the superiority of Western ways of thinking on account of the great advances in science they have spawned, is now slowly realizing that science and materialism do not solve these problems and that the collective wisdom of the ages as gathered in the teachings of Christianity and Buddhism may after all offer insights of greater profundity. Since the problems of man have become global problems, only a philosophy with universal perspectives can offer any guidance.

It is to this end that Japanese philosophers have been trying since the beginning of Japan's period of modernization to reconcile the insights of East and West. Nishida Kitarō (1870–1945) is one who, in works of great interest and equivalent difficulty, tried to bring together the Western idea of dialectics and the Buddhist concept of *kū*, "the absolute." A contemporary of Nishida was the eminent scholar of Japanese religion Anesaki Masaharu (1873–1950), who wrote in English on Buddhism and Japanese thought. He advanced the idea of identifying Christianity with Buddhism in words written at the turn of the century: "I recognize Christ precisely because I recognize Buddha." Such a sentiment might not satisfy everyone, but the intention behind it—to harmonize through identification—is a basic element in Japanese thought. The traditions of Japanese philosophy have been carried on more recently by Suzuki Daisetsu (1870–1966) and Nakamura Hajime (born, 1912) among others. Their writings, although very dif-

30. *Zazen*—"seated Zen" in other words, meditation—is the discipline that prepares the mind to grasp *satori*, the instantaneous flash of enlightenment that is the essence of Zen Buddhism (*left*). Enlightenment may be the result of meditation over a period of years or it may be the result of a mental jolt received from hearing a riddle such as "listen to the sound of one hand clapping." Because of its connection with breathing exercises, Zen meditation gives rise to therapeutic benefits, and this helps to account for its popularity among those only marginally touched by Buddhism.

31. One of the activities of everyday life in which Buddhism, especially Zen, has left a strong impression is eating. Both the fourth and the sixth principles of the Eightfold Path impinge on food, the fourth in its proscription on the taking of the lives of others and the sixth for its concern about how we discipline our own life. In monasteries and nunneries, a considerable proportion of which belong to the Zen sect, a vegetarian diet is the rule. The vegetarian meal shown in this photograph was prepared at the Donke-in, a Zen nunnery in Kyoto, to commemorate the death of the nunnery's founder. Buddhist notions concerning food have affected most forms of traditional Japanese cooking. There are, in addition, a number of restaurants throughout Japan specializing in vegetarian food such as beans, vegetables, seaweed, and above all the extremely nutritious *tōfu* (bean curd).

This animal satire of Buddhism is from the *Chōjū giga*, a scroll thought to be by the Tendai monk Kakuyū (1053–1140).

Literature and Buddhist Inspiration

Just as the Japanese philosophical tradition depends for a large part on Buddhism, so too does its literature. The very form of the written Japanese language is a consequence of Buddhist influence. *Kana*, the native Japanese syllabary, was traditionally thought to have been created by the great Buddhist innovator Kūkai at the beginning of the ninth century and was certainly modeled on Sanskrit. Printing too had early and important connections with Buddhism. Its arrival in Japan came only a half century or so after the formal recognition of Buddhism by the imperial court in 552. The possibility of printing sutras must have given a great boost to the spread of the religion—for example, in 770 the empress Shōtoku ordered that a million copies of a written Buddhist "charm" be printed. So close indeed became the connection between Buddhism and printing that, until the end of the sixteenth century and the introduction of movable type and woodblock printing, virtually all secular work was kept in manuscript form, the printing presses being reserved for Buddhist texts.

There is hardly any form of literature from the Heian period on that does not bear the imprint of Buddhist sensibilities. One of the greatest works of popular literature, the twelfth-century *Tales of Times Now Past* (*Konjaku monogatari*), consists of a thousand stories, many of them Buddhist parables, from India and China as well as Japan. These stories reflect the social values of Buddhism at work in the society of the time, and they exercised a profound in-

fluence on succeeding generations as an instrument of moral education. Literature of a more aristocratic kind too betrayed strong Buddhist influence. That great literary statement of the values most cherished by the Japanese, the *Essays in Idleness* by the monk Yoshida Kenkō (1283?–1350?), is deeply imbued with Buddhist concepts such as that of impermanence: "If man were never to fade away like the dews of Adashino, never to vanish like the smoke over Toribeyama, but lingered on forever in the world, how things would lose their power to move us!"

In later centuries, Buddhism's influence on Japanese literature continued to be strong. In the Edo period it was never far from the center of the literary stage, whether it was being satyrized or being woven realistically into works of fiction. Buddhism made its appearance in the kabuki dramas of Chikamatsu Monzaemon (1653–1724), whose love suicides often died reciting the Pure Land invocation, *Namu Amida butsu*, while for poets who wrote in the seventeen-syllable *haiku* genre like the great Bashō (1644–94) and Issa (1763–1828) the Buddhist view of the world was their view of the world. Issa, for example, expresses in this *haiku* the compassionate nature of the Buddha toward all sentient beings:

> Where there are flies,
> There are human beings,
> There are Buddhas.

Zen and Its Aesthetic

Of all the types of Buddhism, it was Zen in particular that appealed to the *haiku* poets. Zen indeed cast its spell not only over literature but also over the visual arts; indeed, it inspired some of the greatest creations of Japanese art and architecture as well as cultural expressions such as the tea ceremony (*chanoyu*) and flower arrangement (*ikebana*). Zen has its martial aspect too (as can be seen in some of the popular modern martial arts), and it was this that had made it attractive to the ruling warrior class in the Kamakura period in the thirteenth century.

In what ways did Zen affect Japanese art? The application of the ideals of Zen to Japanese aesthetics can be seen in the concept of *ma*, which means "space." *Ma* originates in the idea of controlled breathing. It can refer to blank spaces in a painting, the pauses in *nō* drama, or a part of a house; it is not space as a defined area but is flexible and unframed like the "rooms" in a Japanese house, which have instead of walls easily removable partitions. This concept can be seen, for example, in the tea ceremony, in flower arrangement, and in ink painting (pls. 32, 33). It is at the basis too of intellectual Buddhism, in the use of the idea

Dōgen—portraits form an important part of Zen.

we have already mentioned of *kū*, "the absolute" or "nothingness," as a symbol not of chaos but of the infinite potential of the universe itself.

Zen has its origins in the meditative tradition of Indian Buddhism, but it was in China, where it came into contact with Taoist metaphysics, that Zen developed into a school of Buddhism. From its earliest days in China in the sixth and seventh centuries, Zen has always rejected sutras and statues and stressed the sudden, direct, and immediate nature of enlightenment. It was first brought to Japan as an independent school of Buddhism by Eisai (1141–1215), who introduced the Rinzai form of Zen, which makes use of riddles, disputational nonsequiturs, in order to jolt the questioner into perceiving enlightenment. Another form of Zen, Sōtō Zen, which was introduced to Japan by Dōgen (1200–1253), emphasizes the importance of meditation. Dōgen, like so many other religious innovators of the time, had studied on Mount Hiei, but he left the great Tendai temple for China, where he came under the influence of the Chinese abbot Rujing. On his return to Japan, he took issue with Eisai and exhorted his disciples to concentrate on the discipline of meditation as a means of attaining enlightenment (pl. 30).

Eisai and Dōgen were the founding fathers of Zen in Japan. After them there followed many great religious leaders, poets, statesmen, and especially artists, all of them adherents of the Zen tradition of Buddhism. The Zen influence on ink painting, to be seen in the works of masters like Sesshū (1420–1506), is well known. It should not, however, be thought that Zen was the only strain of Japanese Buddhism to affect the arts. Buddhism—all forms of Buddhism, in fact—played a role in relation to Japanese art similar to that of Christianity to Western art. Buddhism was the generator of the visual arts; Buddhism provided the themes with which the Japanese artistic talent could be realized. The great scroll paintings, Pure Land paintings, and mandalas (representations of the Buddhist cosmos) are all examples of how Buddhism provided Japanese artists with a form of inspiration. And in sculpture the same applies: the peerless tradition of Japanese sculpture, which we will examine from a religious point of view in the next chapter, owes its very existence to the fact that Buddhism allowed it a channel of expression.

Landscape of Four Seasons: Summer, a hanging scroll by Sesshū.

32. Although tea had first been brought from China to Japan in the Nara period, it was as a result of Eisai's fervent advocacy of tea drinking that the habit first caught on. It remained limited, however, to monasteries and the court until at least the sixteenth century. The modern ritualized celebration of the act of drinking tea traces its origins to Sen no Rikyū (1522–91), who formed out of tea drinking an art and a way of thinking based on the ideal of *wabi*, simplicity and stillness. This is cultivated by the careful and exact repetition of movements made elegant, movements such that of drawing water by means of a bamboo ladle. Each stage of the process—including even the manner of holding the tea cup itself, usually of unglazed pottery, casually but convincingly beautiful—represents the adornment of the everyday acts of life with grace and beauty.

33. The configuration of rocks and gravel at the Daitoku-ji (*right*), one of the most famous Zen temples in Kyoto, illustrates the use of *ma*, or space, to convey the Buddhist view of the universe. With their native love of nature, reflected in Shinto, the Japanese created gardens in accordance with Zen ideals, gardens that embody the belief that the totality of nature is an expression of Buddhist law and that the body of Buddha is immanent in mountains, rivers, rocks, and trees. Gardening itself became an art in Japan, and in this way the world of every day and the presence of the Buddha are united. Since even one small stone can suffice to express this idea, the tiniest garden of gravel—containing a world of meaning—can be created in the oddest of places, such as under the emergency staircase in a modern high-rise office building.

8 The Buddhist Pantheon

The various attitudes . . . of the holy images all have their source in Buddha's love, and one may attain buddhahood at the sight of them. Thus the secrets of the sutras and commentaries can be depicted in art. . . . Art is what reveals to us the state of perfection.

Kūkai

Buddhist Images and Their Impact

Books on Japanese Buddhism tend to stress the multitude of sects and the points of difference in their teachings. For ordinary Japanese people, however, there is another side to Buddhism, one that is both more immediate and more all-embracing. It is captured by the poet Bashō in one of his most famous poems:

> Chrysanthemum scent,
> The ancient town of Nara
> And many Buddhas.

The first direct knowledge most Japanese people had of Buddhism was probably gained through looking at statues rather than listening to sutras, through inspiration from beautiful works of art rather than from sermons and philosophy. Images and rituals impressed the popular eye to a far greater degree than doctrines and dogmas impressed the popular ear, not least because of the late development and the difficulty of the written Japanese language, with its almost total dependence on Chinese characters for Buddhist terminology.

As we saw in the last chapter, Buddhism provided the Japanese with a means as well as an aesthetic terminology with which to express themselves in art. The Japanese had, since ancient times, possessed a feeling of the divine in their *kami*, their native gods, who filled them with wonder and awe at the power and beneficence of nature. Now that feeling was spontaneously imparted to Buddhist art, making it Japanese as well as Buddhist.

Every temple in Japan has its own image, or *butsuzō*, a statue of one of the members of the Buddhist pantheon. Many of the ancient and famous temples of Nara and Kyoto and Kamakura (the administrative center of the nation from 1185 to 1332) have a great number of statues of a venerable age and of a beauty that can be universally appreciated. All over the country they are to be found, not only inside the main temple building but also at temple gates, along pathways inside the temple precincts, and in their own special pavilion. Who do these images—some grotesque and terrifying, others peaceful and benign—represent? With a little study, it is not hard to identify the main types and, as a consequence, see not merely works of art but a pantheon of Buddhist deities, objects of worship and of popular devotion. This pantheon can be divided into deities of four types—Buddhas, bodhisattvas, vanquishers of evil, and heavenly guardians—each of which has its own distinct function and is well represented among the images that the visitor to Japan is likely to see in the most celebrated temples.

The Buddhas—*Nyorai*

The Japanese word *nyorai* is a translation of the Sanskrit *tathagata*, a term which is used to refer to Buddha as "the enlightened one." Each *nyorai* is both a separate Buddha with an independent identity and at the same time the concept of Buddha conceived of from different points of view. The most popular Buddhas in Japan are Shaka, Yakushi, Amida, and Dainichi, their names being either transliterations or translations of the Sanskrit. They are the four most "influential" Buddhas.

Shaka (short for Shakamuni, the "wise man" of the Shakas) is the name of the clan into which the historical Buddha was born, and it became the name by which he was known. The number of images of Shaka corresponds to his importance—indeed, in some cases primacy—in the Buddhist pantheon. Images of Shaka have a basic, recognizable stylization, displaying similar features taken from the thirty-two distinguishing marks of the body of the historical Buddha. While not all can be depicted on works of art, certain among them are prominent—for example, the "wisdom protuberance" at the crown of the head, the three rings of flesh around the neck, long earlobes, and the light-emitting curl between the eyebrows, each of which symbolizes one of the ideals that Shaka represents. Shaka's skin is always golden colored, a fact which accounts for the preference for gold in Buddhist imagery in general, and on the soles of his feet are the imprints of a wheel representing the energy of the cosmos, now the universally accepted symbol of Buddhism (pl. 35).

More widely worshiped in Japan than Shaka is Amida,

whose cult centers on his Western Paradise, the Pure Land, and whose great statue in Kamakura is one of the largest and most beautiful of Buddhist images in Japan (pl. 20). One of the beliefs involving Amida was that he had nine forms or manifestations matching the nine levels of nirvana, the function of each of these manifestations being to receive the souls of the dead into the appropriate "heaven." Consequently, from early times Amida has been linked with death and the dead, as he still is now.

Yakushi is the lord of the World of Pure Emerald in the East (the Eastern Paradise) and the Buddha of healing. He offers mankind the benefits of material prosperity and longevity, in contrast with Amida, whose main concern is for the souls of the departed. His role as the patron deity of healing and medicine is the result of twelve promises he made to relieve mankind of suffering and sickness and dispel all spiritual confusion.

Dainichi is a Japanese development of Vairocana, the cosmic, solar Buddha, who was worshiped as the only, the all-powerful Buddha in the esoteric school of Japanese Buddhism and even identified with the sun goddess of Shinto.

The Bodhisattvas—*Bosatsu*

Next in rank to the Buddhas are the bodhisattvas (*bosatsu*), who have found enlightenment but are postponing their entry into nirvana in order to help others find salvation. There is no limit to the number of bodhisattvas, a fact which made it possible for local divinities to be incorporated into the Buddhist pantheon.

Many bodhisattvas have seen their fortunes rise and fall over the centuries. Miroku is one whose popularity attained its zenith early in the history of Japanese Buddhism and later declined somewhat. Miroku derives from the Chinese pronunciation for the Sanskrit Maitreya, who is one of the oldest divinities in the pantheon of Mahayana Buddhism. The belief was once widespread that Miroku would return to earth after many centuries had elapsed to lead all mankind into nirvana (pl. 7).

One of the bodhisattvas whose popularity has remained consistently high is Kannon, who vowed to save all human beings through her own mercy, compassion, and love. Originally Kannon was an attendant to Amida but in time grew to have an independent personality with a female identity—a goddess of mercy. Although Kannon was worshiped early in the history of Japanese Buddhism (Kannon's name appears in the eighth-century *Chronicles of Japan*), impetus was given by the emperor Kameyama (1249–1305), who established a pilgrimage route out of thirty-three temples, with each one representing one of the thirty-three manifestations of Kannon. Numerous pilgrimage circuits of a similar kind were instituted around the country, the most famous being the "thirty-three places of west Japan," Saigoku *sanjūsankasho*. Kannon even became a secret symbol for the Virgin Mary during the Edo period, when Christians were subject to persecution. Statues of Kannon holding a child can be found in many of the places where the "hidden Christians" lived.

Among the manifestations of Kannon that have been most often represented in images are "Kannon with eleven faces" and "Kannon with a thousand hands," representing in their abundance the versatility of Kannon's mercy and suggesting an origin in Indian religious thought. The Sanjūsangendō, "hall of thirty-three bays," in Kyoto houses no fewer than a thousand and one images of Kannon, each with eleven faces and a (hypothetical) thousand hands (pl. 37).

Monju (bodhisattva of supreme wisdom) and Fugen (bodhisattva of teaching, meditation, and the practice of Buddhism) are often found together accompanying Shaka, Monju seated on a lion on the left and Fugen riding an elephant on the right. Nikkō (splendor of the sun) and Gakkō (splendor of the moon) commonly accompany the Buddha Yakushi in a similar capacity as attendants.

The most frequently encountered of all the bodhisattvas and perhaps the best loved is Jizō. Not a major deity in India, Jizō became popular elsewhere once he was absorbed into local cults. His name (Kshitigarbha in Sanskrit) means "womb of the earth," and he became associated in

The main gate of the Tōfuku-ji, a Rinzai temple in Kyoto, is the oldest of its kind, dating from the 1380s.

1. Zōchō-ten (*shitennō*); 2. Taishaku-ten; 3. Misshaku Kongō (*ni-ō*); 4. Gakkō; 5. Fukūkenjaku Kannon; 6. Nikkō; 7. Naraen Kongō (*ni-ō*); 8. Bon-ten; 9. Fudō and acolytes (later works); 10. Tamon-ten (*shitennō*); 11. Jikoku-ten (*shitennō*). Kōmoku-ten, the fourth of the *shitennō*, is concealed from view.

34. This formidable array, at the Hokke-dō in the grounds of the Tō-dai-ji in Nara, appears in all likelihood much as it did in the eighth century, when the statues were created. With its three eyes and eight arms, the central image is a rare example of a supernatural form in Buddhist imagery before the introduction of esoteric doctrines some fifty years later. It is hollow, sculpted from dry lacquer. It stands 3.62 meters high and represents the bodhisattva Kannon. Scholars believe it is the work of Kuni no Kimimaro, the son of an immigrant from Korea.

Kannon's crown contains a solid silver image of Amida. The statues of Nikkō and Gakkō flanking the central image are made of clay and not, like the rest, of dry lacquer; it is thought that originally they were housed elsewhere. Taishaku-ten and Bon-ten, like the other "heavenly kings," are derived from native Indian deities: Taishaku-ten from Indra; and Bon-ten, Brahma. The statues in the Hokke-dō are among the finest works of art of the Nara period.

China with material benefits such as good harvests, long life, prosperity, and rebirth in paradise. Popular Chinese Taoist stories had him making trips to hell to save penitent souls. The images of Jizō are usually made of stone, and they represent him in the form of a priest holding a staff. Through the centuries Jizō has found his way into folklore, nursery rhymes, and popular drama, always as the protector of children. He still holds a high place in Japanese affections.

Myō-ō: Vanquishers of Evil

Perhaps the fiercest and certainly the most famous in this category of deities is Fudō, the principal cultic figure of the sort of Buddhism, described in the following chapter, known as esoteric Buddhism. Images of Fudō are especially common in temples of the Shingon tradition. The *myō-ō* (the name literally means "kings of light") were assigned the task of assisting and serving the Buddhas, Dainichi in particular, and, with their enormous strength, seeking both to vanquish evil and to help human beings resist temptation. The *myō-ō* represent the fearsome and awe-inspiring face of religion, a face which is present in Buddhism as it is in other religions.

Fudō is one of five deities, "the five great kings of light." In his right hand he holds a sword with which to punish the wicked and in his left a rope with which to catch and bind them. Around his head swirls a dramatic mass of flames, which makes him easily recognizable whether as a statue or in mandala paintings. According to one tradition, Fudō took the form of a slave to serve all sentient

Kannon

Dainichi

Shaka

Misshaku Kongō
(*ni-ō*)

Fugen

Monju

beings by destroying evil in the world (pl. 36).

Ten: Heavenly Guardians

These deities, known as *deva* (heavenly kings) in Sanskrit, originated in the native Brahmanism of the Indian people. They predate Buddhism, but Buddhism wisely and effectively turned them into defenders of its faith. The process was similar to the way in which pagan gods in Europe were transformed into Christian saints in order to strengthen the hold of the new faith on the popular imagination.

Most famous in Japan are the "four heavenly kings," *shitennō*, to whom Prince Shōtoku built a temple in Osaka. They have been revered for over two thousand years as guardians of the four directions surrounding the land of Buddha: Tamon-ten protects the north; Zōchō-ten guards the south; Kōmoku-ten, the west; and Jikoku-ten, the east (pl. 34).

As you approach the gate of most large temples, two fierce and forbidding figures appear out of the darkness of their niches in the pillars of the gate. These are the *kongō rikishi*, more popularly known as the "benevolent kings," *ni-ō*. The one on the right has his mouth open; the one on the left, closed. They are the guardians of the temple, protectors of the sacred precincts.

Several of the *ten* are female deities, notably Kisshō-ten and Bensai-ten. Bensai-ten successfully penetrated the world of Japanese folk religion. She became worshiped as one of the "seven deities of luck," and shrines to her can often be seen in the middle of a lake in the precincts of a larger shrine or temple.

Amida

Yakushi

Jizō

Bon-ten

Kisshō-ten

Naraen Kongō
(*ni-ō*)

35. The first image of a Buddha (*left*) for which we have a date is this bronze statue of Shaka and two attendants housed in the Golden Hall of the Hōryū-ji. According to an inscription, the statue was made as an offering for the recovery from an illness of Shōtoku Taishi. However, he died before it was completed, in 623. The sculptor was a man called Tori, a descendant of continental immigrants. Many of the features of the statue—its frontality, the slightly elongated faces, and the symmetrical arrangement of the folds of the drapery among them—are strongly reminiscent of the Chinese sculptural style of the sixth century. The image of Shaka is 86 centimeters high.

36. Esoteric Buddhism was introduced to Japan at the beginning of the Heian period in the ninth century, and from then on representations of Fudō Myō-ō (*right*), the ferocious subjugator of temptation, became a common feature of Japanese art, painting as well as sculpture. This image of Fudō, which is carved from wood, dates from the twelfth century and is housed in the Kongōbu-ji, the head temple of the esoteric Shingon sect on Mount Kōya. The Heian period saw the start too of the widespread use of wood by Japanese sculptors. Wood, with its softer and more natural line, is a material well suited to the Japanese artistic temperament.

37. Work on the 118-meter-long Sanjūsangendo (*right*) in Kyoto was started in 1164, but—what with interruptions caused by war and a ruinous fire in 1249—it was not until a hundred years had elapsed that the 1,001st statue of Kannon was completed. The central, seated image of the bodhisattva is the work of Tankei (1173–1256), one of the leading sculptors of the time. The thousand images, all carved of wood, are smaller and simpler than the central statue and stand about 1.65 meters tall. Although Kannon was still considered a male divinity in the thirteenth century, these statues, with their full round faces and contemplative eyes, embody a feeling of feminine grace and compassion typical of Japanese Buddhist sculpture. The literal way in which faith in the efficacy of large numbers is portrayed here is a characteristic of much of Mahayana art. It is enhanced by the belief that Kannon takes 33 forms to help mortals attain paradise; consequently, these statues can be regarded as 33,033 manifestations of Kannon.

9 Esoteric Buddhism and Shinto

*If a man disciplines himself according to the superior
teaching of Shingon, he will be able to achieve
in this life unsurpassable enlightenment.*

Kūkai

Exoteric and Esoteric

Nowhere is the Buddhist fascination for art and images
more clearly shown than in those schools that are commonly referred to as "esoteric," the Tendai and Shingon
sects, both founded at the start of the Heian period in the
early years of the ninth century. The three hundred years
or so that followed saw a great flowering of Japanese culture, to which Tendai and Shingon, with their beautiful
rituals and exaltation of art, contributed greatly.

Buddhism in Japan is broadly divisible into two types:
"exoteric," or revealed, Buddhism, to which belong those
teachings that can be freely transmitted and understood by
all; and "esoteric," or concealed, Buddhism, whose message
can only be transmitted from teacher to specially chosen
pupil. The Shingon school belongs completely and the
Tendai school partly to the latter type, but all the other
sects are exoteric. While the Tendai school became heavily
impregnated with esoteric practices, the teachings of Saichō, its founder in Japan, are essentially not esoteric, and
it is from them that Zen, Nichiren, and the Pure Land sects
derive much of their inspiration. Nevertheless, the Shingon
and Tendai schools are both central to the Mahayana tradition, and as a consequence they have a lot in common.
Both are syncretic, tending to absorb other currents of
thought and types of worship into their canonical scheme.
Both emphasize the immanence of buddhahood in all
living beings, which, as we have seen, is a cardinal tenet of
Mahayana Buddhism. Both let a preoccupation with ordination and sacerdotal hierarchy disintegrate into nepo-
tism and magical practices.

Saichō and the Tendai School

It was in an attempt to free the court and government of
the influence of powerful and meddlesome Buddhist clerics
that the emperor Kammu moved the capital away from
Nara and founded in 794 the city that later became known
as Kyoto. When a young priest named Saichō (767–822)
settled on Mount Hiei a little way outside the new capital,
his motives were similar: he wished to free Buddhism from
the cloying liturgy, the ceremonial, and the endless disputa-

tion on metaphysical questions that was throttling it in Nara.

In his search for revelation he went to China, where he
studied the Tiantai teachings. These teachings (Tendai is
the Japanese for Tiantai) dwell on the universality of buddhahood, a Mahayana concept that certain of the Nara
schools of thought ignored. Shakamuni (the historical
Buddha) and the *Lotus Sutra*, which contains his last message, are paid particular reverence. Saichō stressed the importance of attaining moral perfection and applying oneself to the service of the nation. His genius lay in his abi-
lities as the architect of a disciplined, monastic way of life.
Although he always took an active interest in different
teachings, including those of the Shingon school, he himself was not an advocate of esoteric practices. After his
death, however, the tradition that he had established in
Japan came under the strong influence of esoteric doctrines. Following a period of consolidation, the great Tendai
monasteries, especially the Enryaku-ji, became centers of
political power, and Tendai monks from Mount Hiei
posed a serious threat to peace. The Enryaku-ji and all the
other monasteries on Mount Hiei were destroyed in 1571,
and, although they were rebuilt, they never recovered
their former importance.

Kūkai and Shingon, the "True Words" School

If Saichō receives credit for the first major break with the
Buddhism of Nara, to Kūkai (774–835) must go the credit
for producing a mature form of esoteric Buddhism and
for generating the basis of integration with Shinto. When
he was young, Kūkai had studied at the seminaries of Nara
and had become familiar with both Confucianism and
Taoism. After finishing his studies he returned for a time
to his native Shikoku, a mountainous island of great natural beauty. A love and longing for nature—mountains and
sea, but in particular the mountains—formed an essential
part of Kūkai's religious outlook (as it did that of Saichō),
and there in the mountains of Shikoku, he contemplated
how truth might best be expressed for the Japanese. If
truth were indeed one and indivisible, as his philosophical mind was inclined to believe, then reconciliation be-

tween the great Chinese systems and the native Japanese intuition into the nature of the universe had to be possible. In an early work, *Indications to the Three Teachings*, he declared in words typical of the Japanese religious outlook: "To guide different types of people, there are three teachings: Buddhism, Taoism, and Confucianism. Although their profoundness varies, they are still the teachings of the sages."

During his trip to China, from 804 to 806, Kūkai collected manuscripts, sutras, and mandalas and became a master of the secret rituals. He integrated two separate branches of esoteric Buddhism: one, called *taizōkai* (world of embryonic truth), taught that there was truth inherent in man; the other, *kongōkai* (world of unshakeable truth), that Buddhism cultivates the supreme wisdom in man through secret words and actions. Nara-period Buddhism had tended toward a reliance on the chanting of sutras. Kūkai, on the other hand, practiced solemn, mysterious rituals, many of them of Indian origin, the purpose of which was to develop the realization of the truth inherent in man. Reduced to simple terms, Kūkai's belief was that rituals could aid man to achieve buddhahood in this world while still alive. The notion that it was unnecessary to undergo an apparently endless chain of death and rebirth is an example of the general simplification of Buddhist doctrine that became a feature of all the later currents of Japanese Buddhism.

Kūkai spent much of his life after his return from China in travels around the country, travels that paved the way for a fusion of mountain Shinto cults with the new esoteric Buddhism. He eventually settled on Mount Kōya, to the south of Nara, where he established a temple and monastery called Kongōbu-ji. The term *kongō* is one of the most significant in esoteric Buddhism. The Chinese characters that in Japanese are pronounced "*kongō*" translate a Sanskrit word referring to a weapon used in ancient India. *Kongō* came to mean a diamond and also a thunderbolt, and it became a Buddhist symbol for the enlightened mind —a weapon that can destroy defilements and pierce to the truth. The word is used in various interesting combinations: *kongō-sui*, "diamond water," is drunk by a novice being administered the esoteric Buddhist baptismal rites and, once initiated, he will develop *kongō-shin*, "diamond mind," to perceive the truth. Kūkai died in 835, but his body is believed to be lying in an uncorrupted state awaiting the return of Miroku, the bodhisattva of the future, when he will rise to life again. After his death Kūkai was given the title of Kōbō Daishi, and it is by this title that he is still best known.

Ryōbu Shinto

The movement called *ryōbu* Shinto (literally, "two-part" Shinto) was made possible by the identification of some principal Buddhist and Shinto figures and by the integration of some of the ideas behind the main rituals of Shinto and esoteric Buddhism. Several characteristics of Kūkai's Shingon school made it amenable to a partial union with Shinto: its syncretism, its veneration of nature,

Kūkai taught the use of mandalas such as the *Daigensui* mandala (these belong to the Tō-ji in Kyoto) for meditation.

38. *Goma*, one of the principal esoteric rites, involves the use of sacred fire to transfer the power of the god Fudō to the priest performing the rite. Small pieces of wood and sanctified oblation instruments are placed on the altar in front of an image of Fudō, and an invocation prescribed by the sutras is intoned. The chanting unites the priest with Fudō, and, when the priest attains the state of mind known as *kongō-shin*, the power of Fudō flows into him and miracles may occur. As the chanting reaches a climax, the fire ignites spontaneously. The priest here is performing the rite of *goma* at the Kongōbu-ji on Mount Kōya. There are many temples where *goma* is performed, but the ceremony at the Narita-san temple, the principal Shingon temple in the east of Japan, is particularly popular. It is held there at nine and eleven o'clock in the morning and at one and again at three in the afternoon.

39. Whereas pilgrimages are open to all believers and the ascetic practices known as *shugendō*—although restricted to men—are performed by laypeople as well as priests, there are certain ascetic rites that can be undertaken by priests alone. One of the most arduous of these is the *sennichi kaihō gyō* (*right*), the "thousand-day austerities around the peak" of Mount Hiei, the center of the Tendai sect. So arduous is it that it has been successfully completed by only eight priests since World War II. The last of the eight and the oldest—he was forty-six when he started—is the Reverend Sakai Tadao, photographed here while on one of the practices that make up the course. Conducted on one thousand days spread over a period of seven years, it includes a regular forty-kilometer nighttime circuit on foot of sacred sites on Mount Hiei. The course begins with a symbolic funeral (in case the devotee should die during the thousand days), and this is followed later by a formal "entry," in which the priest is required to stand still for nine days without eating, drinking, or sleeping.

and its emphasis on fulfillment in this life, among them. Shinto, for its part, had two features that assisted. First, Shinto existed—as it continues to do to this day—in the unconscious attitudes of the Japanese people toward life, attitudes shaped by the natural environment and the climate; it did not contain a set of written doctrines with which to challenge Buddhism. Secondly, the picture of the universe drawn by Shinto is highly positive. It has nothing to say, for example, on the perplexing issues of suffering and death. Besides this, the Shinto *kami*, in addition to their existence in natural phenomena such as mountain streams and rocks, had come to take on functions and powers more closely attuned to those of the Buddhas and bodhisattvas.

In the century or two after Kūkai's death, a system of identifying Buddhist and Shinto deities evolved. This association was enhanced by the central place in the Shingon pantheon held by Dainichi, the solar, cosmic Buddha, of whom Shakamuni, the historical Buddha, is considered merely a terrestrial manifestation. Dainichi is viewed as the primordial and eternal Buddha from whom all other Buddhas proceed. Because of Dainichi's status as a solar deity, a connection was established with Amaterasu, the sun goddess, who herself is the foremost of the Shinto *kami*.

Shugendō and the Men "Lying in the Mountains"

Kūkai's ideas gave rise to a series of developments in Buddhism and Shinto that caught on among the ascetics of the mountains and came to be known as *shugendō*. The mountain ascetics themselves are called *yamabushi* (men "lying in

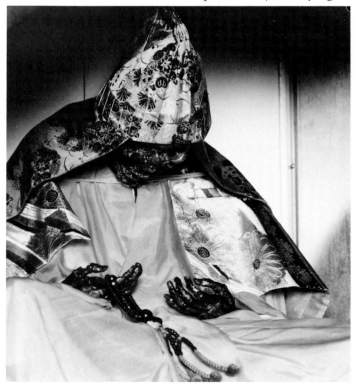

The practice of live burial was banned many years ago, but temples still exist where the remains of devotees are enshrined.

the mountains"). *Yamabushi* had existed in one form or another since the Nara period, if not before. Some of them had colorful backgrounds; maybe they had committed a crime, been involved in an illicit love affair, or reached some impasse in life which forced them to retreat to the mountains either to take refuge or to find time to reflect. They were a mixture of ascetic, hermit, and shaman, and, when Buddhism came to have an influence on their thinking and behavior, *shugendō* was born.

The idea of purification, a fundamental concept and ritual in Shinto, became an important element in *shugendō*. Waterfalls were often regarded as *kami*, and *yamabushi*—and even, sometimes, normal Buddhist monks—would include in their discipline purification under a waterfall. Some of the most holy waterfalls in Japan are to be found in the mountains of the Kumano area in the Kii Peninsula, south of Nara. Kumano also contains one of the most famous pilgrimage circuits, with a history as long as that of *shugendō* itself. The emperor Shirakawa (1053–1125) is said to have gone on pilgrimage to Kumano no less than twenty-four times. The pilgrimage consists of a number of frightening and dramatic rituals and a long walk around seventy-five sacred sites, where prayers are offered or formulas recited.

Pilgrimages were designed for people who wished to gain religious merit and at the same time continue to live in this world. *Shugendō*, however, included more demanding practices reflecting Kūkai's idea of attaining buddhahood in the flesh, an idea that was taken literally by some. There arose a practice, especially associated with the holy Dewa Sanzan (three Dewa mountains) in the north of Japan of seeking instant buddhahood by being buried alive. The training for this, which usually lasted a thousand days, was severe, and some monks died before its completion. Those who did not were buried alive in the posture of meditation. The mummified corpse would then be disinterred, probably after three years and three months had elapsed, and taken to a temple to be worshiped as a Buddha.

Nowadays, although no one is buried alive any more, there are still *yamabushi* as well as pilgrimage circuits open to all (one in Shikoku, of eighty-eight temples associated with Kūkai, is among the most popular). What makes people, even in the twentieth century, wish to go on pilgrimage and to become, if only for a short time, mountain ascetics? The answer may be that the pilgrimage is an ancient and well-tried method of therapy which, with its discipline and prayer and closeness to nature, is no less relevant to modern man and the pressures of urban life than it was to the Japanese of old. Above all perhaps, pilgrims still believe—even if they make their pilgrimage by bus rather than on foot—that they will learn some of the secrets of the world and that this will help them in their quest for religious enlightenment.

10 The Lotus and the New Religions

I will be the pillar of Japan!
I will be the eyes of Japan!
I will be the Great Vessel of Japan!

Nichiren

Postwar Religion and Society

Since the end of World War II several books have appeared in English discussing the phenomenon of what are normally called the "new religions." With titles like *Rush Hour of the Gods* and *Japan's Religious Ferment*, these books depict a mood of crisis—even an apocalyptic situation—in which people are turning to religion out of desperation and anxiety. This approach is tempting but, I would like to suggest, sociologically superficial. The mobility of postwar Japanese society has resulted in great social upheavals, and, while this has led to a weakening in the old *danka* (parish) system, which linked temples and families, it has also served to free Buddhism, to make it more receptive to new developments.

Some of the new Buddhist movements have a history that can be traced back to the turbulent thirties, the era of Japanese militarism, and before. But it was in the postwar era of the war-renouncing Constitution that they experienced their period of greatest growth. The liberalizing policy of the occupation forces played its part. So too did the desire of the war-weary Japanese to build their society along peaceful, democratic, and humanitarian lines. In this quest for a more open society, reenergized forms of Buddhism lent spiritual aid.

Peace, Happiness, and Tradition

Running through the teachings and attitudes of these new movements are a number of common concerns, the most important of which is maintenance of the peace Constitution. The leaders and members of the movements react with suspicion and strong vocal opposition when proposals are advanced to amend the Constitution on matters relating to religion and national defense; they strongly oppose any further militarization, and this is perhaps another reason why calls to the Japanese to increase defense spending have been met with little enthusiasm. Irrespective of political and economic matters, the ingrained suspicion of the people as a whole toward things military as well as the desire to be neutral and to live in peace is not to be underestimated. These are the sentiments of a people who suffered as much under their own military leadership as under allied bombing and who have therefore undertaken never again to take the path of war.

In keeping with the pragmatic optimism found in the spirit of Shinto, the new religions may also be seen as a manifestation of the desire to open a new epoch in Japanese history and to allow the past to fade away quietly and naturally. One way of expressing this desire is in a dramatic reinterpretation of the Buddhist principle of *gense-riyaku*, the attainment of happiness in this life. While the realization of buddhahood in this life is an idea that extends far back into the history of Japanese Buddhism, it has recently come to be understood in rather more material terms, and, allied to the Japanese preference for working for the good of the group, it can probably be considered one of the more important motivating factors behind Japan's postwar economic miracle.

A third common strand that unites the new movements is the desire to preserve what are seen as the positive, traditional values in Japanese culture. Respect for ancestors, for example, is something all the movements support, in part at least as a means of stressing the continuity between them and the older forms of Japanese Buddhism. The new religions are, therefore, perhaps better understood as modern expressions of a religious structure within which man can continue his search for meaning in the nature of life, society, and human spirituality than as religions of crisis.

The Origins of the New Religions

The movements known as the new religions have various backgrounds. Some have Shinto roots—for example, Ōmoto-kyō (founded in 1946), P.L. Kyōdan (Perfect Liberty Association, reformed in 1946), and the older Tenri-kyō, founded by Nakayama Miki in the early nineteenth century although not formally registered as a Shinto group until 1908. Some have Buddhist origins, whereas others are mixed. The three principal Buddhist groups, whose impact has been felt nationwide, share their ancestry in the tradition founded by Nichiren, a tradition that stresses the primacy of the *Lotus Sutra*. Like

40. At the foot of Mount Fuji stands the Taiseki-ji (*left*), head temple for members of Sōka Gakkai. Here on 1 October 1972 a ceremony was held to mark the consecration of a number of new buildings including this enormous hall, known as the Mystic Sanctuary and referred to in English as the Prayer Hall for World Peace. The hall is 30 meters high and 110 meters wide. It covers an area of 7,000 square meters and can seat 6,000 people.

41. Niwano Nikkyō, president of Risshō Kōsei-kai, meets Pope John Paul II at the Vatican. The meeting, the first of several between the two religious leaders, took place on 21 February 1979.

42. People from three continents and as many cultures meet at the Taiseki-ji, with Mount Fuji in the background. Sōka Gakkai, along with Risshō Kōsei-kai and some others of the new religions, has been involved in a process of international expansion. The popularity of these movements abroad stems in large part from the appealing way in which they present the traditional Japanese Buddhist themes of peace and compassion.

Nichiren, they regard this sutra as the principal text of Buddhism, and like Nichiren too they possess a certain controversial spirit. All three of the groups claim that the number of their adherents runs well into the millions. Sōka Gakkai, according to its own estimates, has sixteen million adherents. Risshō Kōsei-kai claims over five million; and Reiyūkai, nearly three million. While these figures may be somewhat exaggerated, they do give an indication of the size of the movements and of their relative strength.

Nichiren and the Lotus Tradition

Nichiren (1222–82) has been likened to a prophet of the Old Testament because of his denunciation of corrupt government, because of the persecution he suffered, and for his dramatic pronouncements. At the age of twenty-one, Nichiren went to Mount Hiei, but he soon became dissatisfied with Tendai rituals and returned to his native Bōsō Peninsula, east of modern Tokyo, and there on Mount Kiyosumi—one early morning at sunrise in the year 1253 —he proclaimed for the first time *Namu myōhō Renge-kyō*, "Hail to the *Lotus Sutra*." This proclamation, known as the *daimoku*, became the rallying call for followers of the Lotus tradition, and that is what it continues to be

Nichiren

to this day. The Tendai school had been known as Lotus (*hokke*) Buddhism up to that time; thereafter, Lotus Buddhism came to refer to the Buddhism of Nichiren and the *daimoku*.

Nichiren began to denounce all other forms of Buddhism: the incantation used by Pure Land believers was the way to hell; Zen was a doctrine of demons; and Shingon rituals led to ruin. Trying to retain the purity of Tendai thought and the Lotus tradition, Nichiren stressed the protection of the nation through a revitalized Buddhism. He interpreted the attempted Mongol invasions of 1274 and 1281 as a form of warning about corruption in the government. "I, Nichiren," he declared, "am the master and lord of the sovereign, as well as of all the Buddhists of other schools. Notwithstanding this, the rulers and the people treat us maliciously.... Therefore... the Mongols are coming to chastise them." Pronouncements such as this, uttered though they were out of deep concern for society and the state, did not win him favor with the military government in Kamakura. He was exiled several times and, before his final exile on wild Sado island in the north of the country, was almost executed—the stay of execution resulting from a miraculous ray of light that appeared just as the executioner was about to do his work. Nichiren's sense of destiny along with his intensity of feeling have been transmitted to the Nichiren movements of today, and so too has a degree of suspicion toward other Buddhist groups.

Reiyūkai, the "Association of Friends of Spirits"

The oldest of the three modern Lotus groups is Reiyūkai, which was founded in 1925 by Kubo Kakutarō (1892–1944). It is based upon a combination of reverence for ancestors and faith in the *Lotus Sutra*, and it includes a certain amount of shamanism and semimagical practices. It was revived after World War II and became a source of stability and inspiration in the years of chaos immediately after the war for people trying to discover a new pattern for society at a time of great change. It was, however, beset by internal problems, and became weakened because it lacked a clear theoretical basis. Signs of a split had already become apparent earlier, and it was in 1938 that Reiyūkai spawned a new movement, Risshō Kōsei-kai.

Risshō Kōsei-kai

The name Risshō Kōsei-kai has been explained by the movement's founder and president, Niwano Nikkyō, in this way: *risshō* indicates the ideal of establishing righteousness and security for the nation, as taught by Nichiren; *kō* refers to the harmony of believers; *sei* expresses the ideal of attaining buddhahood; and *kai* means "society." The *Lotus Sutra* is the central text, and one important achievement of the movement has been the publication of an English translation.

The main building of Reiyūkai, in Tokyo, is designed to resemble hands joined in prayer.

Risshō Kōsei-kai has added a new dimension to the traditional understanding of the *Lotus Sutra* in the concept it has advanced of the perfection of the individual through altruistic living. Using small counseling groups called *hōza*, it has mined a rich vein of personal spirituality and faith in Buddhism, as the testimony below suggests. It comes from a young woman who was converted from Marxism while sitting in front of an image of Buddha:

> *I placed my hands together in prayer and intoned the* daimoku *wholeheartedly over and over again. I must have been chanting for several hours. Suddenly I realized that, despite having lost my beloved sister and intended husband, I was completely wrapped in the warm compassion of the faintly smiling Buddha.*

It is in ways like this that traditional Japanese values and sentiments are preserved and given an outlet in the modern world through a modernized type of Buddhism. Risshō Kōsei-kai possesses in the thoughts of its founder a well-systematized theoretical basis, and in its work it has shown a concern for social welfare and peace.

Some critics have claimed that Risshō Kōsei-kai—to name but one of the so-called new religions—cannot really be considered Buddhist at all. It is my opinion, however, that they have missed the point and that the ideas of Niwano and the movement that embodies them represent one form of modern Japanese Buddhism. Risshō Kōsei-kai was born out of the Lotus tradition; it has tried to interpret Buddhism in terms of modern thought; and it is a lay movement in keeping with the tendency of Japanese Buddhism to do away with the distinction between priest and layman.

Sōka Gakkai

Probably the best known of the new branches of Lotus Buddhism is Sōka Gakkai ("association of value creation"), which, although founded before the war, was reformed in 1946 and blossomed in the fifties and sixties. During those decades, it moved with a spirit of urgency and aggressiveness that made it the center of controversy both at home and abroad. If Risshō Kōsei-kai is in keeping with the spirit of the times, Sōka Gakkai would seem to be closely in keeping with the spirit of Nichiren himself.

In its beginnings it was based on the values of a conservative morality that could save Japan and the world. This morality starts with an absolute respect for the dignity of human life and with a reformation of the individual, a process styled "human revolution," that takes place within the individual through his own efforts to extend his faith, through Buddhist practice, and through study of the writings of Nichiren. Like Nichiren, Sōka Gakkai rejects other forms of Buddhism, and, again like Nichiren, it has conducted—especially under its second president, Toda Jōsei (1900–1958)—a vigorous and successful program of proselytism. Sōka Gakkai shares its head temple, the Taiseki-ji (pl. 40), with the traditional Nichiren sect, and it regards itself as a lay organization within the sect, claiming legitimacy as the modern representative of the tradition of Nichiren.

Nichiren advocated the ideal of peace and national prosperity through the establishment of "true Buddhism." This ideal inspired Sōka Gakkai to make a debut in national politics in the form of Kōmeitō, the "clean government party." Although the two have since parted ways as a result of the postwar dislike of an admixture of religion and politics, a large amount of interest exists at election time.

The Old Lies Hidden in the New

What attracts people to these new movements? One answer lies in the emphasis they place on how to make traditional values serve the needs of Japan now and in the future. They appeal to the innate streak of conservatism in Japanese people. Despite the trappings of modernity, the basic themes of Buddhism can be heard ringing through.

In an interview with Alvin Toffler, author of *Future Shock* and *The Third Wave*, the president of Risshō Kōsei-kai discussed the three Buddhist principles that he sees as the key to perfection of the human self in the modern world: "all things are impermanent," "nothing has an ego," and "nirvana is peace." By ridding ourselves of illusions and by acknowledging the reality of change and the interrelatedness of all things, the possibility of a peaceful and stable life comes into being. We may strive through our work for a higher standard of living, yet, by recognizing the transient nature of things, we can learn to enjoy life in this world while retaining only a limited attachment to it. Such a philosophy strikes a balance between recognition of the importance of man's material well-being and an excessive preoccupation with material concerns that turns the world into a place of competition and distress. In this way, the Buddhism of modern Japan, so far removed from the shores of distant India, echoes the old message in a new form.

Four Truths for the Twenty-First Century

Recently I came across an excellent example of the integration of Buddhist thought and modern science in a work published in 1980 entitled *The Buddha in the Robot* by Dr. Mori Masahiro of the Tokyo Institute of Technology. The four propositions he advances, based on the concept of "the absolute" that we examined in chapter seven, can be seen as an updated version of the Four Noble Truths of the Gautama Buddha, with which Buddhism began. They present a fitting epilogue to our discussion of Buddhism in modern Japan.

1. There is a basic life-force that informs everything from elementary particles to human beings to societies and to the entire cosmos.

2. This life-force is eternal, and our lives are the result of its workings.

3. It is found in both organic and inorganic matter—not only in people but also in minerals, rocks, and all the phenomena of nature.

4. Man must learn to include among his ancestors all forms of life including the very earliest, not just biological forebears. Life is not simply a brief event. It is one and the same as the cosmic life that through eternity manifests itself as "the absolute," beyond thought and description.

A little abstract? Maybe. But the very name we have given ourselves—"human beings"—should help to remind us of the eternal life of the cosmos and prompt us into an understanding of the universe and our place in it, with the help not only of Buddhism and Shinto but of all religions.

Hōza, the counseling groups that have been one of the reasons behind Risshō Kōsei-kai's success.

Bibliography

A list of further reading; books are entered under the chapter to which they are most relevant.

1 Origins and the Eastward Flow

Bapat, P. V. *2,500 Years of Buddhism*. New Delhi: Government of India Press, 1956.

Ch'en, K. *Buddhism in China: A Historical Survey*. Princeton, N. J.: Princeton University Press, 1964.

Conze, Edward, trans. *Buddhist Scriptures*. London: Penguin, 1959.

de Bary, Wm. Theodore, ed. *The Buddhist Tradition in India, China and Japan*. New York: Random House, 1969.

Ikeda, Daisaku. *The Living Buddha: An Interpretive Biography*. Trans. Burton Watson. New York: Weatherhill, 1975.

Ling, Trevor. *The Buddha*. London: Penguin, 1976.

2 The Japanese Transformation of Buddhism

Anesaki, Masaharu. *History of Japanese Religion*. London: Kegan Paul, Trench and Trübner, 1930.

Earhart, H. Byron. *Religion in the Japanese Experience: Sources and Interpretations*. Belmont, Calif: Wadsworth, 1974.

Eliot, Sir Charles. *Japanese Buddhism*. London: Arnold, 1935.

Katō Bunnō et al., trans. *The Threefold Lotus Sutra*. New York: Weatherhill, 1975.

Kitagawa, Joseph. *Religion in Japanese History*. New York: Columbia University Press, 1966.

Steinilber-Oberlin, E. *The Buddhist Sects of Japan*. Trans. Marc Loge. 1938. Reprint. New York: Gordon Press, 1977.

Visser, M. W. de. *Ancient Buddhism in Japan: Sūtras and Ceremonies in Use in the Seventh and Eighth Centuries A. D., and Their History in Later Times*. Leyden: E. J. Brill, 1935.

3 Traditional Buddhism in Modern Society

Morioka Kiyomi. *Religion in Changing Japanese Society*. Tokyo: University of Tokyo Press, 1975.

Murakami Shigeyoshi. *Japanese Religion in the Modern Century*. Tokyo: University of Tokyo Press, 1980.

Niwa, F. *The Buddha Tree* (novel). Tokyo: Tuttle, 1966.

4 The Buddhist Funeral
5 The Welfare of the Dead

Coates, H. H., and Ishizuka, R. *Honen the Buddhist Saint, His Life and Teaching*. Tokyo: Kodokaku, 1930.

Mitford, Jessica. *The American Way of Death*. New York: Simon and Schuster, 1963.

Okazaki, Jōji. *Pure Land Buddhist Painting*. Trans. E. ten Grotenhuis. Tokyo: Kodansha International, 1977.

6 Buddhism and the Japanese Character

Bellah, Robert N. *Beyond Belief: Essays on Religion in a Post-Traditional World*. New York: Harper and Row, 1970.

Hearn, Lafcadio. *Gleanings in Buddha-Fields*. 1897. Reprint. Tokyo: Tuttle, 1971.

Kahn, Hermann. *The Emerging Japanese Superstate*. Englewood Cliffs, N.J.: Prentice-Hall, 1971.

Moore, Charles A., ed. *The Japanese Mind: Essentials of Japanese Philosophy and Culture*. Honolulu: East-West Center Press, 1967.

Vogel, Ezra. *Japan as No. 1*. Tokyo: Tuttle, 1980.

7 Philosophy, Literature, and Art

Dumoulin, Heinrich. *A History of Zen Buddhism*. Trans. Paul Peachey. New York: Random House, 1963.

Hisamatsu, Shin'ichi. *Zen and the Fine Arts*. Tokyo: Kodansha International, 1971.

Keene, Donald, trans. *Essays in Idleness: The Tsurezuregusa of Kenkō*. New York: Columbia University Press, 1967.

Nakamura, Hajime. *A History of the Development of Japanese Thought*. Tokyo: Kokusai Bunka Shinkokai, 1967.

Nishida, Kitarō. *Intelligibility and the Philosophy of Nothingness*. Trans. R. Schinizinger. Westport, Conn.: Greenwood Press, 1973.

Ury, Marian, trans. *Tales of Times Now Past* (selected stories from *Konjaku monogatari shū*). Berkeley, Calif.: University of California Press, 1979.

Yokoi, Yūhō. *Zen Master Dōgen: An Introduction with Selected Writings*. New York: Weatherhill, 1976.

8 The Buddhist Pantheon

Snellgrove, D. L., ed. *The Image of the Buddha*. Tokyo: Kodansha International, 1978.

Sugiyama, Jirō. *Classic Buddhist Sculpture: The Tempyō Period*. Trans. S. Morse. Tokyo: Kodansha International, forthcoming.

9 Esoteric Buddhism and Shinto

Hakeda, Yoshito S., trans. *Kūkai and His Major Works*. New York: Columbia Univesity Press, 1972..

Picken, Stuart. *Shinto: Japan's Spiritual Roots*. Tokyo: Kodansha International, 1980.

Sawa, Takaaki. *Art in Japanese Esoteric Buddhism*. New York: Weatherhill, 1970.

10 The Lotus and the New Religions

Anesaki, Masaharu. *Nichiren, the Buddhist Prophet*. Cambridge, Mass.: Harvard University Press, 1916.

Hammer, Raymond. *Japan's Religious Ferment*. New York: Oxford University Press, 1962.

Ikeda, Daisaku. *The Human Revolution*. 3 vols. Trans. R. Gage. New York: Weatherhill, 1973–76.

McFarland, H. Neill. *Rush Hour of the Gods*. New York: Macmillan, 1967.

Mori, Masahiro. *The Buddha in the Robot*. Tokyo: Kōsei Publishing Co., 1980.

Niwano, Nikkyō. *A Buddhist Approach to Peace*. Tokyo: Kōsei Publishing Co., 1977.

Toffler, Alvin. *Future Shock*. New York: Random House, 1970.

Index/Glossary

(Numbers in italics refer to color plates and their captions)

定価3,600円
in Japan